Creating Communities in Early Years Settings

Creating Communities in Early Years Settings encourages and supports all early years practitioners who work with children and their families within the Early Years Foundation Stage. Offering advice, ideas and strategies for developing an early learning community, this book provides clear guidance and real-world examples that show how practitioners can provide an excellent, inclusive service to meet the needs of young children and their families, and help them to thrive.

Debbie Chalmers presents innovative and practical ideas to promote progress, development and inclusion, while outlining potential pitfalls and explaining how to identify and cater for individual needs. Chapters cover key topics such as:

- the legal responsibilities of a setting
- inclusion
- parental participation and parent-managed settings
- roles and duties of different staff within a setting
- effective and sensitive communication with colleagues and caregivers
- managing transitions.

Creating Communities in Early Years Settings is designed to support early years practitioners, teachers, teaching assistants, nannies and childminders working with babies and children within the Early Years Foundation Stage. The book will also be of interest to students on early years childcare and education courses from level 2 upwards.

Debbie Chalmers is an early years practitioner, a drama teacher and consultant, and a freelance early years and primary education writer.

Creating Communities in Early Years Settings

Supporting children and families

Debbie Chalmers

LONDON AND NEW YORK

First published 2016
by Routledge
2 Park Square, Milton Park, Abingdon, Oxon OX14 4RN

and by Routledge
711 Third Avenue, New York, NY 10017

Routledge is an imprint of the Taylor & Francis Group, an informa business

© 2016 Debbie Chalmers

The right of Debbie Chalmers to be identified as author of this work has been asserted by her in accordance with sections 77 and 78 of the Copyright, Designs and Patents Act 1988.

All rights reserved. No part of this book may be reprinted or reproduced or utilised in any form or by any electronic, mechanical, or other means, now known or hereafter invented, including photocopying and recording, or in any information storage or retrieval system, without permission in writing from the publishers.

Trademark notice: Product or corporate names may be trademarks or registered trademarks, and are used only for identification and explanation without intent to infringe.

British Library Cataloguing in Publication Data
A catalogue record for this book is available from the British Library

Library of Congress Cataloging in Publication Data
Chalmers, Debbie, 1966– author.
  Creating communities in early years settings : supporting children and families / Debbie Chalmers.
     pages cm
  Includes bibliographical references and index.
  1. Early childhood education—Parent participation. 2. Community and school—United States. 3. Home and school—United States. I. Title.
  LB1139.35.P37C45 2016
  372.21—dc23   2015017280

ISBN: 978-1-138-91728-6 (hbk)
ISBN: 978-1-138-91729-3 (pbk)
ISBN: 978-1-315-68909-8 (ebk)

Typeset in Zapf Humanist
by Keystroke, Station Road, Codsall, Wolverhampton

Contents

Introduction　vii

1　The benefits of parental participation　1

2　Ensuring inclusion for all families　11

3　A parent-managed setting as a part of the community　23

4　Making the setting a safe and supportive environment　37

5　Understanding and promoting children's development　55

6　Recording children's progress and achievements　73

7　The responsibilities of a key person　84

8　The roles and duties of different staff within a setting　97

9　Sensitive management of staff, colleagues and clients　108

10　Handling transitions and moving on　130

References and further reading　139

Index　142

Introduction

The years from birth to five are the most vital period for children's development. Their experiences during these early years should provide the secure attachments and the strong foundation upon which they can build to ensure future progress, achievements and success.

Although children's parents and other primary carers at home are of paramount importance, the early years settings that they attend also make an enormous contribution to ensuring that they can achieve their full potential. Whether these are day nurseries, nursery schools, nursery classes, pre-schools, playgroups, crêches, children's centres or childminders' home-based settings, they must celebrate diversity, communicate effectively and work in partnership with families to provide high quality care and learning opportunities appropriate to each child's individual needs.

Most children will attend at least one early years setting for a number of hours each week during the foundation stage, where their families may access guidance, support and new opportunities. The staff, environment and ethos of each setting must be safe, healthy, caring, stimulating, inclusive and welcoming, with policies in place to ensure that everybody is equally respected and valued. This is a huge task and commitment, but one that is carried out every day by the skilled and dedicated professionals who work in early years.

When the conditions are right, early years settings may truly become learning communities that benefit all families and practitioners, encouraging them to work and play together, so that all may thrive and move forward to a bright future.

The benefits of parental participation

There are many benefits of parental participation in the activities of an early years setting, for children, parents and staff. Children are happier, more settled and able to achieve at a higher level when all of their carers share and integrate co-operatively. If settings and homes work together, both parents and practitioners know that their children are accessing the best experiences.

A learning community is a place in which children and their families, carers and practitioners can work and play together to support each other in developing increasing skills and confidence. Working with parents, carers and families is an opportunity for practitioners to share excellent childcare and education practice and to extend learning further into the community.

When parents and practitioners feel comfortable talking to each other, forming constructive, friendly and professional relationships, parents are more likely to co-operate to solve a problem; to offer help; to come in for advice; and to support their children's other carers consistently. When parents are involved in their children's learning, the children learn and progress more quickly. Both adults and children also benefit from improved relationships and gain greater confidence, which creates a happier experience for everyone.

Encouraging involvement

There are many ways in which parents may participate in the activities of an early years setting, to help to promote their children's learning and development, and early years practitioners should always encourage this. An open door policy, which allows parents to spend time with their children in the setting whenever they wish, enables parents and practitioners to spend

The benefits of parental participation

quality time together and to feel more relaxed and able to get to know one another. Setting staff should invite parents into the setting at specific times and for special events, but let them know that they are also welcome to stay whenever it suits them.

It may not be practical to allow parents completely free access throughout the day. For example, it may not be possible to accommodate them within the setting while the children are eating lunch or taking a nap, unless they are prepared to be included in a rota to take a turn to help with some domestic tasks, such as washing up, cleaning tables or sweeping floors. But they should always feel welcome to stay during free flow playtimes to read stories, play games, draw pictures, build models or take part in physical, construction or small world play.

When parents see the activities on offer and absorb the atmosphere and expectations of the setting, they may more fully understand how and why they should play and talk with their children, and can develop a new understanding of how children learn and the wide range of ability levels that all fall within the normal range of development. They may be inspired to provide more quality play and learning experiences at home, to meet a child's needs appropriately and to avoid unrealistic expectations or unhelpful teaching methods.

This may reduce the numbers of children entering settings who have learned to write their names in capital letters or developed a habit of forming

Figure 1.1 Parents should feel welcome to stay at the setting with their children to read stories and play games.

some letters backwards, who have developed no independence skills in putting on their own clothes or shoes or using the toilet, who have no experience of observing acceptable table manners or of using a knife, fork or spoon, who shout and demand instead of asking for what they want and who have no idea how to share toys or adult attention with their peers. Parents who are doing too much or too little for their children can be helped to understand how to gradually move them to a more appropriate level of independence.

Practitioners may often observe children while they feel more confident and settled if a parent is present with them, and also notice the various parenting styles and relationships between parents and children, while proving that they are proud to display and share the care and guidance they offer within their setting. This can be a good opportunity to demonstrate appropriate methods of positive discipline and how to encourage children to get on with their siblings and other children, through parallel or shared play, negotiation and group work. Children will settle more happily into a routine of shared care if they see that all the adults in their lives have good relationships with each other and work together. Consistency between the home and the early years setting is crucial for a child's happiness, development and well-being.

An early years setting can encourage parents and other primary carers to participate in activities by giving them regular information and asking for their support. There could be letters describing events at the beginning and end of each term and at any other appropriate times, information included within the brochures and policies that parents are given, regular informal questionnaires and a variety of notices on the welcome board near the front door. However, it is important to be aware of any families who cannot access information in this way, due to language or literacy needs.

> Practitioners were concerned that a child never seemed to be prepared for activities or events or to have the clothes or equipment she needed. Clearly, messages were not being received by her family and communication between setting and home was not effective.
>
> Her key person greeted her Granny, who was her primary carer, at the end of a session and chatted with her, explaining that the children were going to perform a play and asking if she could provide a plain

The benefits of parental participation

> t-shirt for the child to wear. She also warmly invited her to watch the play the following week. Granny responded eagerly and said that she could not understand the newsletters or notices because she had never learned to read fluently, but, if somebody would tell her what was needed, she would always try to supply the right things for her granddaughter and she would love to come and watch if she really would be welcome.
>
> The child was delighted to be praised by her key person when she brought in her t-shirt the very next day. She was thrilled when her Granny came to watch the play and her working mother was able to re-arrange her schedule and come too.

If staff greet children and their parents and carers warmly and say goodbye personally every day, all family members will come to feel comfortable about arriving and leaving and also confident that they know who they can talk to about anything and that they are able to do so easily. Staff should find the beginnings and ends of sessions good times to make themselves available to talk and they will then be ideally placed to answer questions and queries and to give information and enough notice and reminders of forthcoming events to parents.

Conversations between parents and practitioners are vital and should happen naturally when they choose to stay to help at the setting or to play with their children and whenever there is an opportunity for a friendly chat. Parents will be able to share information about their children's current interests and latest achievements, which may be influenced by siblings, friends, other settings, groups or clubs, family members or other carers, and they may wish to ask for guidance regarding any issues or concerns in areas of health, development or discipline.

Following interests and choosing themes

Early years practitioners should include children's interests in their planning, as they learn more when they are stimulated and engaged. Themes and topics can come from one or more children and will usually also be enjoyed by many of their peers.

Practitioners need to find out, and then make a note of and remember, which special skills and abilities parents have and what experiences they could offer, or whether they would like to help in the setting more often than any allotted rota times they may be given. Armed with that knowledge, it is very important to thank parents for each piece of help they give or offer, to accept all reasonable offers of help promptly and to take them up within a sensible time, sticking to the times and schedules that are arranged and agreed together. It is also important to remember to thank them warmly for their time and effort at the end of each session and to encourage the children to say thank you too, perhaps by making some pictures, clapping their hands or singing a song.

Parents can also be asked for more ideas on how to develop themes. They might be able to think of specific special activities, events to attend or outings to appropriate places, or come in to talk to the group of children and show them things. They may have a van of interesting tools, a police car, uniform and equipment, a traditional sari and veil that they could demonstrate or they could possibly bring in small animals or birds, well-behaved cats or dogs, or a guide dog or hearing dog. Some parents or other relatives might like to lead some cooking with small groups of children, especially of traditional food from other cultures or foods for special occasions.

Parents and carers should feel that their occupations, skills, talents and hobbies are valued. Children are interested in people's costumes, uniforms, equipment and animals and in seeing the things that people have made or photographs of them. They enjoy watching demonstrations of skills, such as how to build a low wall, bath a baby or mend a bicycle puncture. They find it stimulating to work with other adults who are experts in their own fields and can lead activities such as painting and drawing, needlework, collage, tie dying, pottery, modelling, music, singing, dance, drama, gardening, cookery or any sport.

If any parents own farms, allotments or large fruit and vegetable gardens, it may be possible to arrange to take the children there. If they work in factories or on building sites, in zoos or wildlife parks, in museums or art galleries or at country parks or forests, they may be able to arrange for the children to visit.

Planning events to suit family patterns

It is necessary to find out about the working patterns and other commitments of the children's parents and which other forms of childcare are used by families, so that events can be planned to suit as many parents and families as possible. Offering activities at different times and on different days of the week or different parts of the weekend should allow a large number to be involved, at least occasionally.

It is valuable to plan events which whole families can be invited to attend, but some parents might prefer to leave a baby, a child with special needs or an older relative with a carer, so planned times should take this possibility into account. Nannies and childminders may be very happy to attend and support events at the setting, but they may have responsibilities to other children and families that they have to take into equal account when planning their time, so as much notice as possible will be appreciated.

Separated or divorced parents who share parental responsibility, custody and access should both feel welcome to attend and participate, whether they prefer to come together or to take turns to be there. Any parent who is unable to participate in person in any activities could be offered the opportunity to appoint another family member or a nanny or childminder to do so on their behalf, to express the parent's opinions and to show notes, photographs or anything else relevant.

Offering a range of different times for more formal consultations with parents and guardians can be successful in accommodating the needs of almost all clients and mean that most choose to attend. Working parents often need appointments late enough in the evening, while single parents and those with babies may prefer to speak privately with their child's key person before or after a session, or during a morning that their child attends the setting. People also need a choice of days of the week and more than a week's notice of such an appointment.

Practitioners must always be prepared to make themselves available for these extra hours at certain times of the year, to promote the full involvement of families in their children's learning and development.

Considering individual needs

It is important when making any arrangements to consider the individual needs of the children and families within the group. There may be allergies or intolerances that would prevent some children from taking part in certain types of cookery or from being present if animals entered the setting. Some parents may also have strong preferences that their children do not engage in

The benefits of parental participation

particular activities, for cultural or religious or any other personal reasons. Parents must be kept informed of plans for the setting and encouraged to talk to staff if they have any particular wishes or concerns.

Simple adaptations or extra care and sensitivity around a particular child or group of children is often all that is needed to make an activity possible or to reassure a parent and allay their concerns. If a child has particular needs and would be unable to take part safely in an activity or visit without one-to-one support from an adult, consider whether the appropriate key person would be able to offer this if enough staff were available, or whether a parent or other relative or carer would prefer to be present and take responsibility themselves, to avoid the child missing out on the experience.

While taking care to be fully inclusive, practitioners must also respect parents' wishes and feelings. If they say politely but firmly that they prefer their child not to take part in a particular activity, learn about a certain topic or participate in an outing, they should be thanked for their honesty and reassured that the child will be given other things to do or advised that they will need to make other arrangements for their child on the day of the trip. Adults have different ideas, hold different opinions and see things in different ways, usually due to their various situations, beliefs and personalities, and neither parent nor practitioner should become frustrated or consider that the other is wrong, but accept each other's rights and viewpoints in a mature and tolerant manner.

If the practitioners within a setting agree that a child is feeling left out or unhappy and missing out on valuable activities and experiences due to a parent refusing to allow participation too frequently, they need to talk about why they think this is happening. A parent may be over-protective or under-confident for a variety of reasons and may just need a chat, some encouragement or an invitation to take part alongside the child to gradually improve the situation. More complex reasons may require sympathetic and sensitive handling or a particular approach tailored to a family's needs.

If a family makes no effort to participate in any community activity, staff should consider all possible reasons for this. They might be too busy, over-worked and stressed, struggling financially but unwilling to admit that they are worried about paying a requested contribution or shy and nervous about meeting new people and other families. It is also possible that they may have a language barrier or another communication difficulty, an illness, a disability or special needs of their own to consider. A trusted practitioner can help by explaining and talking activities through, identifying potential problems and

The benefits of parental participation

finding solutions, welcoming in another relative or friend who can translate or provide support, or helping families to befriend each other at the setting.

Some parents may be naturally more reserved and prefer to avoid large group social situations. This must be respected, but, after appropriate explanations and reassurance, they may be willing to allow their children to attend some events without them, either with a friend's family or just with the setting staff. This may be the best outcome for these children as it will allow them to be as sociable as they wish and to continue to develop their own confidence within group situations.

Constructive links between home and setting

Practitioners should encourage all families to follow up the setting's activities at home. By showing photographs, making displays and sending out letters and information sheets, they can make parents feel that it would be fun to participate in their children's learning and development in this way. When talking to parents, setting staff can tell them which activities their children enjoyed most and which helped them to develop new skills. They may offer

Figure 1.2 Encourage families to offer their children's favourite activities at home.

materials to take or to borrow, or lists of the recycled or easily available resources needed, along with instructions and suppliers.

It is important that families are helped to understand that simple household items have at least as much value as potential tools for play and learning as expensive new toys and that they can be less limiting. Young children love to use their parents' or grandparents' pens and pencils to make marks in notebooks and on lists. They are fascinated by helping to unload the grocery shopping and, with appropriate supervision, can be permitted to build towers and models with the tins; shake boxes and packets to discover which make a good sound; and compare items to decide which are heavy and which are light. They can also be encouraged to help to sort the clean washing, matching socks and putting clothes into piles for various members of the family. Participating in improvised activities such as these can promote spontaneous, child-initiated learning, develop imagination and build strong and close relationships between young children and their parents and carers.

Children should be encouraged to ask their families to help them to re-create some of their favourite experiences from the setting at home and parents should be supported as they try to do this. If they are unsure, they could be offered opportunities to come into the setting to watch or help with various activities until they become more skilled and confident and understand how to provide quality learning experiences at home and why they need to do this.

Staff may also set an example which encourages parents and carers to improve their children's independence and manipulative skills in specific areas by demonstrating how they are allowed to help with activities such as preparing their own snacks. Pouring drinks, spreading toast and cutting fruit develop fine motor skills in an enjoyable and productive way and promote sharing and social interactions. Practitioners could invite families to become involved by donating fruit to the setting for snack times and also allow them to come in and watch the children preparing their snacks if this would help them to feel more confident about re-creating the experience at home.

If they have opportunities to ask questions within a relaxed atmosphere and to join in with activities and events, parents can become more confident and develop new or improved skills to offer to the setting and in their parenting. This can create happier home relationships and increased self-esteem for parents and children. Constructive links between home and setting

The benefits of parental participation

ensure children's needs are met and preferences and interests known and respected. It also benefits the setting staff, as they enjoy improved relationships with parents, finding them more supportive and co-operative, willing to be involved and less concerned about very minor problems and grievances. Children supported consistently by their parents are secure and confident, ready to learn and develop and more able to get on with other children and adults in their early years settings.

Ensuring inclusion for all families

It is of vital importance that all practitioners are seen to be fully inclusive and prepared to treat all children and everybody who cares for them with equal respect. Of course, this will not mean treating them as though they are the same, but respecting their differences and celebrating their diversity. Although all staff must participate fully in this, one or more practitioners within each setting will be particularly responsible for ensuring that individual needs are being met. These are known as Equal Opportunities Co-ordinators, Equal Needs Co-ordinators or Equality Named Co-ordinators and commonly referred to as ENCOs.

Practitioners should adapt their speech to be appropriate when speaking to children, parents, grandparents, other relatives and friends or professional carers. Information may need to be delivered in certain ways to some parents, while other carers may need to have things written down so that they may pass them on to parents later. Nannies and childminders may be able and willing to contribute a great deal to a child's profile and appreciate times set aside to speak privately and honestly with the appropriate key person at a setting about a child and family.

It is useful to make comparisons with the normative stages of development that all children pass through, to allow a child's individual progress to be monitored and extra support offered if any developmental delay or very high ability is identified. But it is important not to compare children directly with each other, as all children develop at their own individual rates and in different areas at different times. Inclusive practice values this diversity and encourages children to be themselves.

Ensuring inclusion for all families

Figure 2.1 Allow each child time and space to develop as an individual.

Cultural diversity

Children attending early years settings may have a variety of nationalities, cultures, religions and parenting styles and practitioners must aim to respect and include them all fully. This will entail taking careful note of any foods a child may not eat for religious reasons, such as pork, any clothing or jewellery that they should not remove or any words that they should not hear or say, and observing these preferences just as they observe all children's allergies and intolerances.

Unless the setting has a particular religious ethos, it should aim to educate children about a variety of festivals and beliefs, such as Christmas and Easter, Divali, Hanukkah, Eid and Ramadan, mentioning Christianity, Judaism, Islam, Hinduism, Sikhism and others. This may be achieved through telling and acting out stories, showing pictures, singing songs and playing games. Practitioners should place no emphasis on any particular religion, making it clear to children that some people believe in each, and also respect the fact that some families wish their children to follow no religion at all. Learning about festivals celebrated in other countries, such as the Chinese New Year, can also be interesting, fun and valuable for all children.

Families may be willing to share information, stories, songs, objects, pictures or photographs to explain their particular religious festivals, but must understand that their role in this situation is to educate, and not to impose a belief upon others. Practitioners should ensure that any precious items are not left at the setting or handled by children without supervision.

It is necessary to be aware of any festival that a particular child may not celebrate. For example, if there are Jehovah's Witness children in the setting, they may be given a special job with a staff member in another room if the group is singing to a child on their birthday, and parents may prefer to keep them out of the setting during Christmas celebrations such as parties and concerts.

Practical matters

It is a good idea to mention small matters to parents informally, such as a toilet training child's need for simple clothes, because dungarees, tight skirts or tights under trousers make some accidents inevitable when a child is learning. However, it is very important to respect parents' wishes to dress their children in the way they would in their own countries and to help the children to learn to manage independently.

Children of some faiths, especially girls, must keep their bodies covered or get changed privately from a young age. Boys and girls may wear caps or turbans or other head or hair coverings. Appropriate facilities must always be sensitively offered to accommodate these needs. Children need to learn to recognise for themselves whether foods are safe or permitted, with support from adults, and to ask when they are not sure. This applies equally to children with allergies or intolerances and to children with preferences for religious or cultural reasons.

Practitioners must guide children safely and sensitively in all of these areas, seeking to educate all families and interest them in each other, in order to create a diverse community that works and plays happily both together and alongside each other and in which all individual needs are valued and treated with equal respect.

Overcoming language barriers

When there is a language barrier, practitioners should try to learn a few crucial words in the home languages to help children who do not yet understand

Ensuring inclusion for all families

Figure 2.2 Dolls and other toys within a setting must reflect diversity within the community.

English and they may use mimes and signs too. They must find out who can interpret for particular children and ask whether any family member or other carer can access written information in English, or if they would like to have things read out to them or to take copies home to someone who will translate privately and in their own time.

> When a Japanese child first began to attend a pre-school, her mother was learning to speak and understand English but could not yet read or write it. If staff needed to ask a question, they asked the child or her older brother to translate for their mother and then to repeat her answer in English. If permission forms or payments were needed, they gave her the written information and time to take them home to her husband, who could read and write fluently in English and interpret all the information for her, so that she understood what she was returning to the setting. When she brought them back and offered them with a few words of English, she was thanked warmly in simple English phrases which she understood.
>
> The mother was inspired to work hard at learning English and was soon able to speak and understand more confidently, which made her much happier and able to participate in the setting's activities. A year later, she offered to come into the pre-school on a regular basis to cook traditional Japanese dishes with the children and was able to explain what she was doing and answer their questions in English. She told staff that she was pleased to be able to give something back to the setting which had given so much to her and to her child.

When some parents go to work abroad, their spouses or partners, who are extremely intelligent, professionally qualified and highly respected in their home countries, may suddenly find themselves isolated and frustrated as they leave behind the stimulation of their own work, family and friends and try to care for their children in an unfamiliar place which uses a language that they do not yet speak or understand. If they are offered appropriate understanding and support, which respects their feelings and their intelligence, they will be able to quickly achieve proficiency in the language and then begin to share valuable skills and regain their independence and self-esteem.

> When an Arabic child joined a nursery, her father wrote out a list of the words she used for simple requests (spelt out in phonetic English) and it was kept inside the door of a staff cupboard, where all practitioners could refer to it easily during sessions. They tried to memorise this list and use the words alongside English words and signs, but also aimed to help the child to acquire an English vocabulary through the use of simple words combined with signs and lots of repetition. Both the child and her parents responded to the challenge with enthusiasm and quickly learned to use basic English.

When a parent or carer cannot speak English fluently, it is important to make efforts to communicate through using a few words in their first language and then offering them simple, useful words that they might remember. Practitioners should include them courteously in speeches made to groups of parents, but make sure that they also speak to them personally later and clarify how much they understood.

All children and their families should be helped and supported in the learning of English throughout their time at a British early years setting, but their home languages must also be respected. If there are any parents who speak the same first language as each other within a setting's clients, staff could consider introducing them and possibly suggesting that they may be able to offer support to each other. Even if they do not seem very compatible, they might be willing to assist each other at times when translations are needed.

> Amongst the children of a pre-school was one child who was Russian. His parents spoke English fluently, so were able to communicate through letters and telephone calls, but they were both in full-time work. He was cared for by a nanny who spoke only Russian and German. At the age of three, the child could already translate quite efficiently for his nanny, but did not always agree to do so.
>
> When the child's mother informed staff that the nanny would like to spend some mornings helping out at the pre-school, they considered

> ways in which they might be able to communicate with her. None of the practitioners could speak or understand Russian but some of them had some previous knowledge of German, so they used an English/German dictionary to remind them of vocabulary and were able to find the words they needed to speak to the nanny, so that they could all communicate on a basic level. She appreciated this effort so much that she tried hard to match it by remembering a few of the English words that were used frequently, which also helped her within her day-to-day life while she was caring for the child and his older siblings in England.

Making or buying signs, notices and labels in a variety of languages and displaying them around the setting makes all families feel welcome. An ENCO might make notices, using coloured cards and pictures cut from catalogues, to label each area and activity in a setting, such as: outside, role play, mark making, small world play, construction, art and craft, books and computer. Each family and staff member can then be asked to write the words onto the sheets in any languages they know. Many parents and carers may be inspired by this project that invites them to make a unique contribution and arrive in the mornings with lists prepared, that have been gathered from all members of their families. When the sheets are finally finished and laminated, they may contain words in more than twenty different languages and dialects, from Arabic to Finnish, and all of the families will take pride in seeing them displayed around the setting.

If British practitioners try to copy some of the words that are written from right to left, such as Arabic and Hebrew, or in other symbols, such as Chinese and Japanese, they can gain a fuller understanding of how difficult it is for parents who use these languages to learn to read and write in English, however intelligent they are and however fluently they may have learned to speak it.

Parents and children with disabilities and special needs

When settings include children with disabilities or special educational needs, they will need to create appropriate individual learning plans and liaise with other professionals as necessary. Practitioners must always be willing to help parents to access any services and additional aid available to them and to apply for anything that could help them or their children.

Parents with physical disabilities should be able to access the provision without difficulty. This will involve having wide opening doors, ramps if necessary, a disabled toilet and parking close to at least one entrance. If the premises are on more than one level, a lift should be available or all children, staff and services made available to disabled parents on the ground floor. For parents who are partially sighted, notices can be made bigger or staff can describe everything verbally. They can also sensitively guide them around the setting and hand all of their children's possessions to them, rather than expecting them to look for them within a busy playroom or crowded cloakroom area. It is very important to be deaf aware and to sign or mime for those with partial hearing, attracting their attention before speaking slowly and clearly while facing them.

> One pre-school child had an English father and a mother who was French and deaf. This mother could speak and lip-read competently in both French and English and also use sign language. Staff were sensitive to her needs and willing to use any of these themselves, as she preferred. Before the age of four, her daughter could speak both languages fluently and expressively and also sign rapidly to her mother and her little brother, who was pre-verbal but already communicating through signs. The mother being deaf helped the whole family to become tri-lingual.

Allergies and intolerances must be observed in parents as well as in children, including reactions to foods, flowers, grass and substances that can exacerbate skin conditions. It is very important to avoid potential allergens and it should always be possible to arrange for a parent who is helping out or performing a rota duty in a setting to swap tasks with a member of staff, if they are unable to prepare the children's snack, or to touch the playdough, the sand or the water or to spend prolonged periods in the garden.

Within settings, children need to work with adults who are enthusiastic and interested in embracing experiences, but some parents can, at times, transmit their feelings of anxiety or dislike of certain activities or materials. To avoid this happening, parents who are less confident or not comfortable with paint, clay,

Ensuring inclusion for all families

water, sand, mud, gardening, crafts or baking should have the support of an experienced practitioner working alongside them. Those who have low levels of literacy or English fluency should not be asked to read stories to the children, unless they choose to use the pictures to tell a story of their own.

Classes, courses, training and learning to support each other

The local early years team will usually offer parenting classes and family learning days, on themes such as cookery or messy play, in local premises. Staff in settings nearby can encourage those families who would most benefit to take part. Sometimes, it is practical to invite parents to join setting staff on an appropriate training course, such as first aid.

Within their settings, practitioners will encourage parents to play and learn alongside their children and then to try out activities at home. They might also suggest and lend books for them to read and courses for them to attend. If a

Figure 2.3 Local family learning days are very valuable for encouraging friendly and respectful interactions between staff, children and families.

family suffers a tragedy or goes through a difficult experience, their key person or the manager of the setting might approach other parents who have been through something similar in the past and ask if they might introduce them to each other, so that they could offer support.

At an early years setting, staff will encourage friendships amongst parents and children to enable them to support each other and to find more pleasure in attending the setting and learning together. If there is a waiting room or cloakroom area in which parents can gather before and after sessions, this can help to encourage social skills, confidence and friendships. Through maintaining an ethos of respect for everybody, it is possible to break down barriers caused by lack of language fluency, disabilities and special needs, culture differences or lack of confidence.

> When two families of Finnish speakers were introduced to each other by nursery staff, the mother who was still hesitant in English became much more confident once she had made friends with the fully bilingual mother. She was prepared to try new things and join in with many activities, knowing that she could explain to someone easily and get help if she became confused. She was transformed from a nervous person, who had appeared shy and under-confident, to an outgoing, friendly and very supportive parent, once she was able to reveal her true personality.

If practitioners take care to ensure that fathers, grandmothers and grandfathers feel at least as welcome as mothers and nannies when they attend events or volunteer to be rota helpers, there need be no shortage of them in the setting. Childminders and nannies should always be introduced to each other, as they usually have more in common with each other than with the parents and enjoy a chat about their work. It is good to be able to offer the use of the premises for regular childminders' meetings or play sessions, especially during holidays if the group meets only in term times, but, in a community-shared setting which is hired out to other groups, it can be tricky to find the time and money to do this.

Formal courses, classes and workshop sessions can be provided to ensure that the early years environment remains a learning community for parents as well as children. It is important to try to avoid barriers forming that could affect parental involvement by asking when most parents would be free to attend, varying the times and days and giving enough notice and reminders. It is good practice to offer two copies of letters for separated parents or parents and childminder and to find ways to subsidise courses or access funding so that they are cheap or free to parents. Some barriers to attendance may be removed by providing a crèche, or running classes while children attend their usual early years sessions and by allowing breast-fed babies to attend with their mothers.

Settings may be unable to offer as many workshops and courses as some clients would like, especially if they operate as a shared setting in a busy community hall and have no supernumerary staff; but practitioners should be fully aware of all resources available in the local area, so that they may still offer advice and information. When parents have a need that a setting cannot personally meet, its staff should know where else they might go to find something suitable, even if it is to another village or into the nearest town or city.

Benefits for families throughout the Early Years Foundation Stage

Clients may join an early years setting if they need full-time or sessional care with appropriate education and social opportunities for their children, many of whom will go on to local schools together. For most families, this will be on regular days each week, while parents work or fulfil other commitments. However, any family can suffer a sudden emergency, such as the hospitalisation of another child or relative or a crisis at work, requiring extra hours or travelling, and will appreciate their setting offering extra sessions and support in this situation. Some flexibility regarding numbers and times should be included within a setting's policies wherever possible to allow staff to respond to the needs of families in this way.

Research studies have found that early years settings can benefit parents as well as children by encouraging them to make new friends or join other groups, to become involved in their children's schools, to work to set up events and activities, to bring about local changes, to offer mutual help and exchange to each other, to try out new things with their children at home and to study or find jobs.

Some of this research is featured in the book:

- *Early Childhood Learning Communities – Sociocultural research in practice* (Fleer, Edwards, Kennedy, Ridgway, Robbins and Surman, 2006)

The book was published by Pearson Australia and draws on Australian research, sociocultural theory and the principles of Reggio Emilia in Italy, sharing research findings important in an evidence-based approach to pedagogy practice.

There are also many interesting and useful articles to be found online, including:

- 'Developing understanding of the idea of communities of learners' (Rogoff; Taylor & Francis online; 1994)
- 'Everyday family and community life and children's naturally occurring learning opportunities' (Dunst, Hamby, Trivette, Raab and Brunder; Sage journals online; 2000)

An early years learning community is successful if it brings people together to make friends and forms a supportive social network, offers help and advice as well as listening and encouragement, increases parental skills and confidence, demonstrates good childcare skills and learning opportunities and arranges activities and trips that are both educational and fun. It must welcome everybody, include all children and their whole families and celebrate diversity, whilst always striving to meet individual needs and to offer a good and positive experience for all.

A parent-managed setting as a part of the community

Some pre-schools, crêches and nurseries are run and managed by committees of parents. Children, parents and staff can benefit from being a part of this type of early years setting. Children can achieve and progress more easily if parents are involved in making the decisions that affect their daily care experiences, as this enables them to have a greater understanding of what their children are learning and how to provide quality experiences at home.

When parents take a greater interest in their children's learning and development and have some influence and control over the running of the early years setting, they feel happier about their children's attendance and find it easier to be supportive. Offering their skills to the committee increases their involvement and shows the setting how much they are valued as their children's first educators. They may also find opportunities to develop new skills, alongside staff or other parents, allowing them to manage activities and events or go on to further work or training themselves.

Offering skills and projects

If parents are encouraged to share their hobbies and interests, and knowledge and skills, an early years setting may be able to offer a wider range of experiences, which more accurately reflect the home lives and outside interests of the children. The children will also have opportunities to see that their parents consider learning to be important and that they continue to learn in their adult lives, through involvement in a range of activities. While they develop their abilities to work successfully with other people in this situation and help to shape the setting, parents will gain in experience and self-confidence.

A parent-managed setting as a part of the community

This may enable them to enjoy their roles as parents more fully and also to seek to become involved in other community activities beyond the settings that their children attend.

Staff will benefit from increased support from parents and their expertise on their own children, as they share information and insights. They will be able to plan activities to extend the knowledge and experiences children already have, and to be sure of their individual needs, interests and preferences. Also, they may more easily ask parents to help and to share skills and experiences when they have already taken on the job of being a committee member or officer for the setting. Parents can be asked to help staff with general or specific tasks and to share the workload of running the setting at times. Involving a range of people helps staff to see the early years setting as an integral and vital part of the community.

A parent management committee contributes to the community development role of the early years setting when parents, along with staff, identify needs in their local community and try to meet them. They are able to make friends and to work together to organise and run events for the wider community to attend. In accordance with their Equal Opportunities policy, parents will welcome all families equally, respecting their different cultures and backgrounds and helping them to learn to respect each other. Children benefit from this, as they learn to value diversity from an early age and to celebrate it within our society.

Small-scale projects devised and initiated by parents should always be encouraged and can sometimes grow into much bigger projects that benefit the community for years to come. For example, in many villages there will be a parent and toddler group, set up and organised by a small group of friends, which meets weekly, either in people's houses or in a village hall. If this group grows larger, or if a parent expresses an interest in setting up play sessions in hired premises that could be open to all village families, a pre-school parent committee may decide to contribute to the cost of hire and materials and recognise the group as an affiliated toddler group. This group can then benefit from advice and support from qualified practitioners and is more likely to thrive and successfully meet the needs of all its parents and children.

> Parents who were members of a pre-school parent committee and also attended play sessions with their younger children in one village chose

> to take over the running of a local toddler group and, in consultation with the parent committee, run the two groups simultaneously, sharing ideas and resources. Some of the pre-school practitioners were asked to take turns to lead the toddler group sessions, with the help of a rota of parents. Toys and equipment were regularly swapped and shared and parents found that their children were able to move easily from the toddler group to the pre-school when they reached the appropriate age.

Providing regular opportunities for parents and their youngest children to meet, talk and play together, before the children are old enough to attend a pre-school, can mean that parents make some friends and are better prepared for the next stage of their children's lives. Parents attending with their first child will be able to seek the advice of others who already have older children and glean a greater understanding of what will be required when they join the pre-school and eventually a primary school. Children who have already been exposed to playing within a group and have learned to take turns and to share resources and adult attention from a very early age will be better able to cope with the transition to pre-school when they begin to attend without their parents. They are more likely to understand how to function independently within their peer group and relate to the other children, and are less likely to be upset or confused by the level of noise and busy activity going on around them.

Sometimes, parents who run toddler sessions do so because they are already qualified or very experienced in childcare themselves. Others may have less experience but quickly find that they enjoy the work and choose to go on to study for a childcare or education qualification when their children grow older. They may eventually take up a position in an early years setting or a school. In this way, leading sessions for other parents while caring for their own young children can provide either a route back into work or a whole new career. Alternatively, parents may eventually return to work in other professions as their children grow older, but also become governors of their local schools or members of steering committees or organisations for their villages or areas. They will have moved from helping out at a few community sessions to planning and organising projects and motivating large numbers of people within the community.

A parent-managed setting as a part of the community

Figure 3.1 Children can learn to share and take turns by playing with others from a very early age.

The parent management committee

In most settings, a parent committee will consist of between five and twelve members, three of whom will be the officers, as follows.

The **chairperson** leads the committee and chairs the business meetings and annual general meetings. He or she also deals with the recruitment and employment of staff for the setting when necessary. This involves advertising for and interviewing potential new staff, checking qualifications, obtaining references and applying for enhanced Disclosure and Barring Service (DBS) disclosures. After contracts have been signed and practitioners have joined the staff team, the chairperson will work in conjunction with the manager of the setting throughout their employment, carrying out staff appraisals, identifying training needs, and, if necessary, using disciplinary procedures.

The chairperson will take the lead in ensuring that the committee observes equal opportunities when considering applications from disabled practitioners and interviewing potential new staff. If appropriate, adjustments could be made to allow people with disabilities, sensory impairments or individual needs to carry out the job effectively, without compromising children's safety or limiting their experiences: they must be considered on an equal basis with non-disabled applicants.

The **treasurer** administers bank accounts and systems for collecting fees, handling invoices and paying staff salaries through PAYE. He or she also takes in money from donations and other sources, applies for grants, authorises the spending of funds, pays bills, takes information from financial statements and produces annual accounts and budgets, oversees a petty cash system and presents an up-to-date written statement of accounts at each meeting.

The **secretary** prepares an agenda for each meeting, takes the minutes during a meeting and types them up as a report to be presented at the next meeting, writes an annual report and writes and receives letters on behalf of the setting. He or she also arranges appropriate insurance cover and issues contracts for work to be done.

Between two and nine further members may be elected to the committee. They will share out the other tasks between them, such as encouraging fundraising, organising events, arranging donations or prizes, seeking publicity, updating information, and amending policies and procedures or developing new ones. More members may be co-opted onto the committee if it is agreed that this is necessary or would be beneficial to the setting.

The parent management committee has overall responsibility for and control of the running of the setting. They make all necessary decisions regarding the admission and withdrawal of children. They may buy, rent or lease land and buildings and maintain them for the use of the staff and children, or sell them and keep some funds in reserve. They are required to belong to the Pre-School Learning Alliance (PLA), to send a representative to attend and vote at their meetings, and to take out all necessary insurance policies to cover the premises and everybody using them during the hours that the pre-school is in session.

The committee is also responsible for the day-to-day management of the setting and for keeping records and registration forms for all children, as well as daily attendance registers, a first aid kit, an accident book, a visitors' book, and information on staff and children's allergies, intolerances, preferences and individual needs. However, these duties will usually be delegated to the manager and supervisors of the setting. Together, the adult team will organise social activities, special events and outings for parents and children.

Committee members must know or find out what equipment is needed to provide a good early years curriculum and arrange to obtain, make or buy it, and to maintain it. Parents must be encouraged to share their skills in sewing,

A parent-managed setting as a part of the community

painting, woodwork and DIY to maintain the premises and the equipment. The committee must take every possible opportunity to involve the wider community in the work of the setting.

Sharing information

New families placing their children at the setting should receive a brochure that contains details of session times, contact numbers, fees, free funded hours, other sources of funding, childcare vouchers, dates of terms and holidays, names of staff and their roles and qualifications, aims, principles, rules and ethos of the setting, and policies on illness, accidents and other important issues. The brochure will also describe the other procedures that contribute to the day-to-day running of the setting.

Before helping at a session, a parent, nanny, childminder or other carer or guardian will have the necessary rules explained to them by a staff member. For example, they must understand that anything they see or hear is confidential

Figure 3.2 A brochure must be prepared for the families choosing to place their children in a setting.

and must only be shared with a child's key person or the manager. They must also observe health and safety regulations regarding a younger child accompanying them, maintain high standards of hygiene if preparing a snack for the children, remember to keep hot drinks away from the children, and avoid taking children to the toilet.

A notice board near the entrance, or in a place where parents wait to deliver or collect their children, can hold all the day-to-day messages, reminders of forthcoming events, thanks for previous support, and advertisements for anything outside session times that staff think may be of interest to families. Newsletters given out or sent by post or email to each family should ensure that everybody receives important information when they need it.

The staff and the parent management committee will also request information from each family when their child joins the setting. Staff need to know the children's full names and what they are to be called, their dates of birth, addresses, contact telephone numbers and details of parents or guardians and other regular carers, contact details for their doctors, emergency contact numbers, and details of all people authorised to collect the child, with a password for security. It is also essential to record details of siblings and pets, other settings attended, the children's first languages and which others are spoken at home, all immunisations and any major illnesses, operations or hospital stays, chronic or recurring medical conditions, disabilities or health problems, allergies or intolerances, special requests or circumstances affecting any child and any special or additional needs.

Parents or guardians need to give signed permission for staff to seek medical help or an ambulance for children if necessary and may choose to give permission for staff to take photographs within the setting and for children to be taken off the premises for short local walks from time to time. Standard forms should be given to all families so that these permissions may be obtained.

Sometimes, members of the parent committee will hold extra information about a child or family, or make special arrangements for payment, and not all staff will be informed. They may also plan events or fundraising projects with some or all staff, but not disclose details to other parents until they are sure that they can go ahead successfully.

Information may be shared between the parent management committee and the staff of a setting in various ways. The manager will attend the committee meetings and take information, ideas and decisions from staff to committee members and from the committee back to the staff team. Copies of all written plans and proposals will be shown to staff before they are implemented.

The chairperson, treasurer, secretary and other committee members may discuss ideas, opinions, issues and projects with staff when bringing or collecting their children, or they may arrange to attend parts of some staff meetings to share discussions. A manager might often hold a short meeting, resolve a few issues or attend to other business with one or more of the officers during or immediately before or after a session, while other staff care for their children within the setting.

At consultations, each key person will inform committee members of the progress of their own children, but they may also make some general statements about the progress of the group of children as a whole, indicating that it is generally good, or that there are some whose progress is slow or exceptionally quick. This allows the committee to be sure that the staff are aware of individual children and meeting their needs, without breaching confidentiality by discussing particular children.

The parent management committee can share information with the other parents and carers of a setting by asking staff to include their contributions in newsletters and in notes on the notice board, or by compiling their own letters and handing them out themselves. They should invite all parents to their annual general meetings and offer them opportunities to speak and indicate their opinions.

Committee members should make themselves known to the other parents and spend time talking to them when bringing their children to sessions or waiting to collect them and at social and special events. In this way, they may easily check whether they are happy with the service provided or find out what else they could do to improve the experience for families. The committee should always ensure that working parents who seldom collect their own children from the setting know how to contact the chairperson if they wish, either directly or through the setting manager.

Policies and procedures

A policy is an aim agreed on and adopted by a party, such as a committee, while a procedure is a series of actions conducted in a certain order. In accordance with the guidance of the PLA, a parent committee should consult with staff and parents regularly, listen to their ideas and suggestions, value their opinions and deal promptly and effectively with any issues that are causing them concern.

There will be policies for such areas as health and safety, healthy eating, sickness, access to outdoor play, a suitable and varied curriculum, children's toilets, employment of staff and the role of a parent helper. There will be agreed procedures for first aid, preparation of children's snacks, fire drills, children arriving and leaving, setting up and tidying up of children's play areas, dealing with parents' complaints and new staff inductions. Policies and procedures may be written by one or more staff members or committee members to be checked and agreed by the rest of the adult team.

When a policy or procedure is decided, the committee should be aware of national legislation and guidance and make every attempt to follow it, taking advice from experts when unsure. It is necessary to continuously check that policies are still appropriate and adequate for purpose and to amend them if they are not. Procedures should also be updated regularly, as circumstances may change and there may then be a better way of achieving the same result.

New policies may be introduced at any time and the committee should check whether staff need any further training to be able to implement them confidently. Guidelines and recommendations for the early years change continuously and staff must have opportunities for continuing professional development, in order to be aware of each new idea and requirement. The manager or staff members themselves may identify a need for further training in specific areas, or it may become obvious during an appraisal. Some staff may need support to update or upgrade qualifications. Adequate staffing, time, space and facilities must always be in place and be reviewed regularly.

It is an essential requirement that the names of all committee members are given to the Office for Standards in Education (Ofsted) and that Ofsted is notifed promptly of all changes. Members and officers may change frequently, but failure to notify Ofsted of every change is a breach of regulations and will adversely affect the grade awarded to the setting at an inspection, regardless of the standard of care and education observed and assessed. Although the parents who are committee members have no unsupervised access to the children and the staff know them well, out-of-date information is considered by Ofsted to be a safeguarding issue.

The staff must work with the parent management committee to ensure that the setting has the financial resources required to implement its plans, policies and procedures through setting fees at an appropriate level and combining these payments with the government funding that they receive for each

A parent-managed setting as a part of the community

Figure 3.3 Informal performances by practitioners and children can raise vital funds and create valuable publicity for settings.

eligible child. They will usually also hold regular fundraising and sponsored events, such as performances, concerts, tombolas, cake sales, auctions and trundles, for which parents, families and friends donate prizes, promises and sponsor money, as well as their time and goodwill to make the events successful. These may have the added benefit of helping to publicise the setting across the local area and attracting new clients.

The committee may also accept donations of money or payment for specific furniture, equipment or supplies from parents and families or their companies and businesses. At times, staff and parents can supply or donate other vital resources to the setting, from paper or unwanted toys, to unused computers or printers, or outgrown spare clothes and boots. Planning should always be based around the equipment and resources that are available or easily obtainable at the time they are needed.

The adult team may decide to apply for grants or funding for specific projects. It is important that some members of the committee and the manager or supervisor of the setting understand how to apply for various sums from both regional and local sources. National grants are also offered at certain times. In most cases, the setting must send a letter of application, with either details of a planned project or of equipment that needs to be replaced or added to, or a set of accounts. Some settings may be linked to other organisations or agencies, such as churches, community associations, housing authorities or voluntary groups. These organisations are likely to make money available to these particular settings, either at regular times or when it is requested.

If the setting is to be a registered charity, it must comply with the requirements of the Charities Act. The trustees must apply to the Charity Commission for the charity to be registered and supply copies of its trusts and any other documents required. The Commission will keep a register of charities, containing their names and particulars. However, a charity whose gross income is below the official limit is exempt from the register, as is one excepted by regulations made by the Secretary of State and whose gross income does not exceed the specified limit in this situation.

Parents joining a setting with their children must clearly understand its aims and ethos, to be sure that it is right for them and to be able to work constructively with its adult team for the good of all the children. As well as getting to know the staff, they must know which parents are members of the committee and who they can contact with a particular issue or query. They must be sure that all business will be conducted honestly, openly and fairly and satisfy legal requirements. Committee members are responsible for making decisions that affect the setting's children and families and must be able to explain and justify their roles and decisions when asked to do so, by staff or other parents.

Parents have the right to be informed of decisions that will affect their children and the provision of their care and education. In order to accept the setting's policies and procedures, they must fully understand the roles and responsibilities of the parent management committee and be willing and able to support its members whenever possible. Making details of the formal constitution and complaints procedure available to all parents can help with this.

Committee members and teamwork

New parents may wish to join the committee themselves, as soon as a position becomes available, and need details of the types and amount of work involved, especially if it also means becoming a trustee for the setting premises or the registered charity. Every parent must know that they have an equal right to stand for election onto the parent management committee and be encouraged to do so if they wish. It is important for parents to remain informed and interested, as new members and officers of the committee are frequently required because each child attends an early years setting for an average of only two years before moving on to the next stage of their education.

Diversity amongst members must be encouraged and, if any significant group of families is under-represented on the committee, parents from those families should be especially encouraged and offered support to join. As far as possible, the parent management committee should always be representative of all families attending the setting.

Effective teamwork occurs when the members of the adult team, both staff and committee members, recognise their needs for interdependence and mutual support. They need to feel committed to their jobs and the setting, and to meeting the goals they set together; but still able to apply their own particular skills and knowledge to achieve success as individuals, for their own personal or professional development and for the good of the organisation.

Appraisals between staff and parent committee members allow everybody to identify any needs for further training or support, changes to be made or areas of concern. A committee may set up both individual and group appraisals, in order to take every person's needs and opinions into account. If all of the adults involved can communicate effectively, they will be able to resolve concerns, issues and problems through discussion in the early stages. They will all feel able to make suggestions confidently and those made are likely to be more constructive. They will make an effort to understand different points of view and work together to resolve conflict and achieve positive results. Open and honest communication between the staff and the parent management committee enables them to work as a team and make their setting an asset to the whole community.

The management committee will be aware of its need and ability to provide personal development opportunities for all parents who want them. Participating in a community activity, such as performing tasks for a pre-school, can encourage parents to feel willing and able to participate in other activities for the wider community, such as becoming a committee member or governor for a school, or a member of a tenants' association or village society.

A parent who joins the management committee may develop a number of new skills. These might include writing agendas, minutes, reports and letters, and presenting information or understanding and using business accounts, statements, invoices, PAYE systems, budgets and financial systems, and plans, policies and decisions. They may develop greater self-confidence through organising and chairing meetings, special events, outings and fundraising activities or by working and negotiating with legal guidelines, insurance companies, social services, councils and local authorities. They may learn a great deal while recruiting and employing staff, from advertising and interviewing to identifying and arranging training, carrying out appraisals, using grievance procedures and working together to provide a high quality early years curriculum.

Gender, class, race, sexuality, disability and background should not be considered when recruiting for committee members, except when striving for diversity and inclusion and trying to ensure fair representation for all groups within the community. All parents have an equal right to become involved. However, any parents who prove themselves unable to carry out duties in an organised and committed way, to be enthusiastic and positive, to work as members of the team and to treat all others with respect must improve through training and support, or resign for the good of the team and the setting.

There are some disadvantages to parent management committees, which can actually hinder community participation in some areas. If some parents are very dominant, they may lead others into swift, safe decisions that prevent new ideas or opinions, block changes and developments and ignore people's needs and feelings. Quieter or less confident people, or those new to the committee, may feel unable or unwilling to speak, offering support for every idea without thinking anything through, take on too much work because they dare not say no, or become confused and uncomfortable. These people are likely to resign from the committee before they have time to share their own skills and may not join other committees and associations in the future. A setting will never adapt to the needs of its families while this situation continues and its client numbers and popularity may suffer.

If people who find it impossible to make decisions or stick to the point serve on parent management committees, they can prevent discussions from moving forward and frustrate other members. Some block every new idea or search for too much information, while some bring in irrelevant points or wider issues at every opportunity. Some people serve on too many committees at once and see each one as a series of procedures, losing sight of the aim or vision of each group and often rushing from one to another until they appear to forget where they are and what they are trying to achieve. They are then unable to offer any positive benefits to the groups they should be enhancing and their places would be more usefully filled by others who have only one or two interests on which to concentrate. These people must be tactfully encouraged to make choices and withdraw from some of their commitments, in order to be more successful in others.

A community may be led and dominated by the same person or group of people for many years, meaning that others' valuable knowledge and skills are lost and the needs and opinions of some groups are ignored. Many strong and hardworking people may not come forward to offer their participation if they feel that they would be unable to work successfully with those who are already running the local groups and committees, or that their ideas would not be valued or taken up. This must be avoided wherever possible, as these people reduce the contribution that their committees make to the families within their community.

In some areas, becoming involved in early years settings can encourage parents to overcome the disadvantages of poverty and social exclusions, replacing them with support networks, self-help groups and people from diverse classes and cultures coming together to build strong communities for themselves. Parent management committees must always seek to embrace positive change and variety and strive to contribute to true community participation.

Making the setting a safe and supportive environment

All early years settings must implement effective policies to ensure equal opportunities for all children and families and to support children with learning difficulties, particular and additional needs, which are usually classified as special educational needs and disabilities (SEND). Providers have an obligation to comply with all legal requirements and legislation relevant to inclusive practice.

Acts, reports and initiatives

In 1978, The Warnock Report suggested that mainstream settings were best for children with special educational needs (SEN). The Warnock Report and Education Act of 1981 introduced statements of SEN for these children. In 1989, The United Nations (UN) Convention on the Rights of the Child stated the rights of disabled children to be educated in mainstream environments, to achieve social integration and individual development. It gave children the right to provision, protection and participation in their own learning. The United Kingdom signed this in 1991.

The Children Act of 1989 described children in need to include those with disabilities. It stated that the welfare of all children was paramount and that local authorities must provide appropriate services and the same rights for disabled and non-disabled children. The Education Act of 1993 led to the Code of Practice for identifying and assessing SEN. The Disability Discrimination Act applied to childcare provision for the first time in 1995, while The Education Act of 1996 laid the foundations for current legislation and statutory guidance.

Making the setting a safe and supportive environment

In 1998, The Human Rights Act stated that no child should be denied the right to education. They should also have rights to privacy, freedom of expression and non-discrimination. The School Standards and Framework Act of 1998 introduced Early Years Development Plans to place all children in relevant provision.

The SEN and Disability Act of 2001 made it against the law from 2002 to discriminate against children in the provision of any service. Local Education Authorities (LEAs), schools and settings had to make adjustments and plan for increased access for disabled pupils. Early years providers had to have a written SEN policy, a SEN Co-ordinator (SENCO) and relevant training for all staff to enable them to follow the SEN Code of Practice.

Further commitment from the Government towards improving expectations and outcomes for all children and young people and overcoming the barriers to learning of SEN, through early intervention and improved partnerships, came through Every Child Matters and Together from the Start in 2003 and Removing Barriers to Achievement and the revised Children Act in 2004. The parents of SEN children were given the right to affordable and appropriate childcare and flexible working hours in 2005, when the Disability Discrimination Act also defined the duties of employers and suppliers of goods and services to the public, schools, local authorities and community education to promote inclusion. The Childcare Act of 2006 required LEAs to provide children's services in an integrated and inclusive manner, offering parental choice and the best start for children, as suggested in the ten year strategy which began in 2004.

In 2007, three priority areas were included within Aiming High for Disabled Children: Better Support for Families. These were: access and empowerment, responsive services and timely support, and improving quality and capacity. Education settings were given new duties to promote discussion on identity and diversity, develop a common vision and make life opportunities available to all.

The Care Standards Act of 2008 appointed the Office for Standards in Education (Ofsted) to regulate daycare and out-of-school care, using fourteen national standards, three of which related specifically to SEN. The Equality Bill of the same year stated a commitment to equality for all individuals, as well as society and the economy.

The Early Years Foundation Stage (EYFS), introduced in September 2008, brought together the Curriculum Guidance for the Foundation Stage of 2000, Birth to Three Matters of 2002 and the National Standards for Under-Eights

Daycare and Childminding of 2003. Working under the guidance of the EYFS, early years practitioners had to recognise every child as a competent learner, able to be resilient, capable, confident and self-assured, and to ensure that each unique child had the right to fully inclusive practice. There were six areas of learning and development, including sixty-nine early learning goals, which practitioners and teachers used for observation and assessment.

The Statutory Framework for the EYFS was revised and introduced as a new set of standards for learning, development and care for children from birth to five years from September 2012. The four themes that underpinned the guidance were: a unique child, positive relationships, enabling environments, and areas of learning and development. There were now three prime areas and four specific areas, including a total of seventeen early learning goals between them, which most children were expected to reach by the end of their foundation or reception year in school.

The particular needs of certain groups of children were recognised, such as SEND, those with English as an additional language (EAL) and those with behavioural, emotional and social disabilities (BESD). Funding for extra staff and resources was made available to ensure provision within early years settings and schools for these children.

The importance of inclusion

Inclusive practice is vitally important in an early years setting. All children, parents and staff need to feel valued and respected, in order to ensure a happy, welcoming environment with equal opportunities, in which all can thrive and make progress. In the past, inclusion was considered to be only relevant to children with particular special needs, but, in more recent years, it has been recognised as being important for all children and their families. A child, parent or carer may be at risk of exclusion for a wide range of reasons, such as physical or mental disablity, emotional or behavioural difficulties, home language, illiteracy, race, age, gender, sexual orientation, religion, social class, unemployment, temporary accommodation, poor quality housing or poverty.

Early years settings should develop their services to fit the needs of their clients, placing children and their families at the centre of their practice by asking them what their needs are, involving them in decisions on policies and procedures, and building on the interests and skills of individuals to personalise learning. Childcare and education settings must conform to health and safety requirements and ensure that they employ the legal number of appropriately qualified and experienced staff, enabling them both to meet correct ratios of adults to children and to appoint a particular staff member to lead in areas such as special and additional educational needs, disability and equal opportunities.

All adults working with or caring for children need to observe the UN Convention on the Rights of the Child, which gives them the right to care and protection, the right to express their views and the right to have these views appropriately considered, taking into account their age and maturity level. For example, in an early years setting, children may have a free choice as to when they take their morning snack and which and how much fruit they choose. They may pour their own drinks, decide when they have had enough, clear the table after themselves and stack their own plates and cups for washing. If a child chooses not to have a snack, or prefers to sit and watch rather than join in with a group game, this choice must be respected and permitted, provided the child does not try to disrupt the safety or enjoyment of the children who do wish to eat or play.

There should be an Equal Opportunities policy to ensure that all children are treated fairly and with equal respect. Both boys and girls must be encouraged to play with all types of toys and in all areas of the setting and adults should ensure that no particular group monopolises certain equipment, games or activities or tries to prevent others from choosing their own play. Positive images of people of all ages, both genders, diverse skin colours, nationalities, religions and cultures and with all kinds of special needs and disabilities must be included within play and display resources and any discriminatory remarks or assumptions made, by an adult or a child, must be challenged and corrected by setting staff. The Equality Named Co-ordinator (ENCO) will lead this area of practice.

If a setting does not comply with the legal requirements for registration, inclusion, care and education of their children, they will not achieve a satisfactory inspection grade from the Ofsted inspectors who make a planned visit or come to inspect following a complaint or concern reported to them. The staff of the setting will then be informed of the alterations and improvements they must make and the timescale allowed for this. If these changes do not occur within the allotted time, or if the provision is judged to be dangerously inadequate, Ofsted can withdraw its registration and force it to close down immediately. In some cases, legal proceedings may be brought against the owners or managers of settings that are judged to have been negligent or against staff members suspected of committing offences.

Safeguarding policies

Policies and procedures must meet the requirements for Safeguarding and Promoting Children's Welfare contained within the Statutory Framework for the EYFS. The setting staff should be aware of all areas of their Health and Safety policy and take care to avoid both direct and unintentional discrimination, as only fully inclusive practice can promote a truly healthy environment.

The setting provider must consider illness and injuries, the good health of children, infection, and appropriate actions to be taken if children fall ill. There must be a Sick Child policy which details how the setting staff will notify Ofsted and local child protection agencies of a child's serious or fatal accident, injury or illness and act upon their advice. It must also describe how a parent or designated carer will be informed of a child's illness or injury and how parents and carers will be informed of the setting's procedure for sick children. Also included will be the requirements for an appropriate number of qualified paediatric first aiders to be on duty at all times and for a suitably stocked and regularly checked first aid box to be kept on site, as well as the procedure for recording all accidents and first aid treatments administered. The provider must inform Ofsted if they consider a child to have a notifiable disease and act on advice from the Health Protection Agency.

A policy on Administering Medicines should state that only prescribed medication will be given, once a child has safely taken the medication at home more than once and is now recovering and well enough to attend the setting. Accepting children into the setting who have chronic medical conditions needing continuous medication requires a risk assessment and a regularly reviewed healthcare plan for each child, devised and agreed by the manager, key person and parents.

If any pets are kept, there must be an Animals on Site policy. This should check that the animals will be safe around young children and not a health risk, that their habitats will be cleaned to a high standard to prevent infection and that anyone touching the animals will then wash their hands.

A Food and Drink policy must ensure that the children's meals, drinks and snacks are healthy, balanced and nutritious and that the people who handle

Making the setting a safe and supportive environment

Figure 4.1 Practitioners must have a policy in place to ensure that pets within a setting present no risk to health or safety.

and prepare food have received food hygiene training. It should remind staff that children must be offered regular drinks and reminded of how they can obtain fresh drinking water at any time. Ofsted must be informed and their advice followed if food poisoning occurs at the setting.

Making the setting a safe and supportive environment

There must also be a Food Hygiene policy which states that information on any child's specific special dietary needs will be recorded, that training should be available to practitioners and that advice should be given to parents and carers on the healthy provision and safe storage of packed lunches, if appropriate. The pre-school environment must be kept free from smoking at all times, inside and outside, through the strict observance of a No Smoking policy by all adults whilst they are on the premises.

Children should be educated about good hygiene practices, such as when and how to wash their hands, and also taught through example, as they see that staff wear gloves for nappy changing and for first aid and that they wash their hands at appropriate times, preferably using foaming soap dispensers and paper towels. Children should be encouraged to blow their own noses and throw away their own tissues, cover their mouths when coughing or sneezing and then wash their hands before touching other people or toys. To maintain a healthy environment, staff must set a consistently good example for children to follow. Any tables or equipment used for both play and food preparation or consumption must be cleaned and sanitised between each separate activity.

Appropriate insurance, such as public liability and employer's liability policies must be in place and renewed yearly. No adult without Disclosure and Barring Service (DBS) clearance may be allowed unsupervised access to children, especially during toileting and intimate care routines. Schools and early years settings must be aware of this requirement and enforce it at all times.

Stringent rules also apply in other sensitive areas, which could potentially be open to abuse, such as photography. The taking of photographs and filming of children's performances and special occasions is only permitted if the parent or guardian of every child involved has given written permission and also only if the pictures, videos or DVDs are recorded by a member of staff or a parent. It is not legal to allow any person from outside the setting to attend for this purpose, unless a DBS check and all appropriate licences have been obtained in advance. The timespan, difficultites and costs involved in doing so mean that it is not a viable option, so, unfortunately, settings cannot always please all families by providing this type of record of events. It is important to be honest about this and give clear explanations in advance, to avoid problems caused by families requesting or offering services that are not permitted.

In an early years setting, the safety of children and adults must always be the first priority. Staff must organise the space, furniture, toys and equipment to create a child-friendly environment, ensuring that children can explore and

Making the setting a safe and supportive environment

Figure 4.2 Adults must encourage children to engage in appropriate risks and challenges, while offering careful and sensitive supervision.

learn as they play, take appropriate risks and meet achievable challenges, whilst always being carefully and sensitively supervised by adults who extend and enhance their opportunities for new learning and greater confidence.

Managing risks

Children must be taught about keeping themselves safe, and encouraged to become aware of risks and potential dangers, in order to gradually develop the abilty to assess risks for themselves and take appropriate action to avoid some whilst overcoming others. Staff must explain possible risks that would be managed by the adults and teach children how to obey instructions without question when this is essential for their safety. For example, children must respond to the signal for a fire drill or evacuation emergency and leave the premises calmly, assemble at the designated meeting point outside, participate in the taking of the register and then re-enter the building safely or wait in an appropriate place with staff until they are collected by their parents and carers.

Specific risk assessments should be carried out to fit various situations, such as the evacuation of children with special needs in the event of a fire or drill,

Making the setting a safe and supportive environment

the supervision of children while they are eating and the opening of the front door to someone not recognised by staff.

Clear procedures must be in place and followed by all staff to ensure that security is adequate. Steps must be taken to make it impossible for children to leave the premises unsupervised, or for anyone to enter and have access to the children without being authorised to do so. Staff must also ensure that children are only collected by their parents and designated carers and, in the case of an unfamiliar or unauthorised person arriving to take a child home, a parent must be contacted to give authorisation before the child is released from the setting.

This applies also in the case of other parents asking to take children home to play with their own children or offering to give children a lift home to their parents. Even if staff know and trust the parents concerned, telephone calls must be made to check that the children's parent intended for this to happen. Parents do sometimes forget to tell staff of arrangements they make with each other, or fail to see the importance of this security measure, but simple telephone calls to ensure children's safety prevents both the confusing and worrying situation of parents rushing in to collect children who have already left the premises with friends and the potentially very serious situation of children being lost or passed to people who should not have access to them.

Sometimes, children's parents have been legally denied access to or contact with them, for reasons such as abuse or mental health difficulties, or because they wish to take the children from the custodial parents. In these cases, a risk assessment may need to be carried out to give all staff a consistent procedure to follow if these parents arrive at the premises. Depending on the level of potential risk to the child or to other children or adults present, staff will need to know whether they should refuse and prevent admission or whether they need to contact the other parent or even the police.

If children are to be taken off the premises for any reason, either on a walk or transported in a vehicle, all parents and guardians must give written permission. Staff must ensure that adult : child ratios are appropriate and legal and take all necessary information and equipment with them, including emergency contact details for all children, a first aid kit, clean drinking water and any child's ongoing medication for a chronic condition or possible allergic reaction. A separate risk assessment must be carried out in advance for each outing and a copy given to each adult accompanying the children on that day.

Risk assessments for outings may be set out in a number of ways, but should include details of the place, date and time of the visit, the name(s) of the organiser(s), the hazards and their risk ratings, which may be classed as low, medium or high. Each hazard should be listed under sub-headings such as environment, groups or journey, and its risk rating noted under two further headings, which detail the likelihood of encountering the problem and how serious the outcome could be if it happened. There should then be details of a control measure to reduce each risk and the new rating that each then attracts. These should all be reduced to low risk whenever possible. Other risk assessments, that are to be used within the setting, will need different headings but may follow a similar format and must record the name of the manager or key person responsible for the child, group or activity.

Appropriate physical contact

Young children need consistent contact with familiar adult carers. They have basic needs which require intimate care routines throughout the day and they have times when they need to be held, hugged or cuddled, taken by the hand or onto a lap, lifted up or carried. Carers must always respond to young children's needs for comfort in these appropriate ways.

Figure 4.3 Carers must always respond appropriately to young children's needs for physical contact and comfort.

Making the setting a safe and supportive environment

In a childcare setting, children have all of these needs and require physical contact for reassurance and security, but some practitioners may worry about the management of this physical contact and how to handle it safely for the children and for themselves. Young children can be helped to respect their bodies by learning the names of body parts and how to describe or point to them, often through songs and rhymes, exploring what they can do when engaged in physical activities and being encouraged to take independent responsibility for self-care from a young age.

Many two-year-olds can go to the toilet and wash their hands without help and all children should learn to eat and drink for themselves as soon as they have developed the right amount of co-ordination within their arms and hands. Staff should explain to children, taking into account their age and level of maturity and understanding, that the children's bodies are their own and they can choose which touches they like and which they don't, with a few obvious exceptions such as essential medical procedures and restraint to prevent them from endangering or injuring themselves or others.

Key messages to offer to children are that they can learn about themselves, make their body do many things, tell people what they like and don't like or if they feel upset or worried, say no to things that feel bad or unsafe and ask for help at home and in their early years setting. They should be reassured that they have people around them who care and that telling a trusted adult if they are worried will help to keep them safe. They may discuss with practitioners which adults make them feel safe as individuals and which professionals help to care for people in the community. Stories, songs and rhymes can help to explain the themes of body parts and safety, as can role play, physical and outdoor play, when sensitively led and monitored by practitioners who are alert for signs of a child's inappropriate knowledge or behaviour.

In order to verbally tell an adult about inappropriate behaviour, young children must have the language skills and know the correct words. But those who are not able to speak clearly may be able to use signs, draw pictures or show an adult what happened using a doll. It is important to use correct anatomical language as much as possible, but very young children will use the names given to body parts and functions within their own family.

Very young or immature children and those with disabilities, special needs or speech delay can be most at risk from potential abusers, as these people will think that the children cannot tell anybody. Staff working with these children must be particularly vigilant in watching for any sign of abuse or inappropriate behaviour learned, and offer alternative communication methods to allow them to tell if they need to. But practitioners should gather evidence carefully and be absolutely sure before making a serious accusation, as it is not always easy to concentrate on facts alone when imagination and emotions are stimulated.

It is important not to frighten children, but to make it clear to them that almost all children have very safe lives with lots of people to care about them and look after them. They need to believe that most adults will protect children from harm and only a very small number would ever hurt a child, so they just need to be careful around strangers and wary of anybody who tries to force them to do things that make them feel uncomfortable or tells them that they must keep secrets.

Child protection procedures

Early years practitioners must, of course, ensure that relevant checks and clearances have been carried out before they are alone with children. These will be requested from the DBS, which took over this task from the Criminal Records Bureau (CRB). They will also access appropriate training as a part of their continuous professional development and form close links with children's families. They must have security measures in place to prevent any unauthorised person from entering the premises uninvited, or having unsupervised contact with the children, and uphold the safe ethos of their individual settings at all times.

Safe recruitment and selection procedures must always be followed when employing a new staff member or accepting a volunteer, to ensure that all adults in the setting are suitable to work with children under five years old. Staff should receive training to enable them to create a protective ethos for both children and staff in their individual setting. To meet the three key commitments of the Alliance Safeguarding Children policy, a setting must build a culture of safety: to protect children, promote awareness of, and respond promptly to, incidents or concerns of abuse or neglect, and empower young children to keep themselves safe.

A Child Protection policy needs to be in place at every setting and all staff members should be aware of it. A designated person, who has received specialist training, should be available to advise the other staff when necessary and all staff should be aware of how to pass information to that person. Other staff should all have regular basic training on child protection procedures and responsibilities.

Making the setting a safe and supportive environment

If children disclose that they are being abused or neglected, or changes in their appearance, play or behaviour lead staff to believe that it is so, each child's key person must discuss what to do with the setting manager and follow the agreed procedure. This could be to make a record of the concerns and details, clearly dated, for the child's confidential files, including what was observed or disclosed, the exact words the child used if they spoke about abuse, the names of the people observing the signs or hearing the disclosures and the names of any other people who were present at the time. A key person should also talk and listen to the child, offering reassurance that action will be taken.

The managers and staff of early years settings should be aware of the procedures to follow to make a referral to the local social care team. Parents are informed at the same time as the referral report is sent, unless a parent is the likely abuser. If this is the case, investigating officers will inform the parents, under the guidance of the Local Safeguarding Children Board (LSCB). Procedures for contacting the local authority on child protection will include keeping a list of social workers' contact details, to make it easy for setting staff and social services to work together in an emergency. Ofsted must also be notified of any incidents or changes in arrangements.

A setting procedure may describe how staff should behave towards each other and the children, offering mutual respect and valuing diversity in skills, ideas and opinions, discussing differences calmly and working together to plan new activities based on the interests of groups and individuals. There should also be clear procedures to follow when arranging one-to-one work or dealing with suspicions or allegations.

There are specific procedures regarding allegations of abuse against staff. Parents must know how to complain about the actions of anyone living or working on the premises. Such allegations are recorded, referred to the social care department and reported to Ofsted. In many circumstances, the member of staff will be suspended on full pay during the investigation for their own protection, although this is not an admission of guilt. If a staff member or volunteer is dismissed due to abusive conduct, the setting's procedure will be to notify the Independent Barring Board to include their name on the list that prevents them from working with children again.

Planning of the rooms in the setting should ensure that staff can always see each other. Curriculum planning can include keeping children safe and making them strong, resilient and listened to, within an environment that respects and values each individual. Suspicions and investigations must remain confidential. Supportive relationships need to be formed with families and should be maintained even during investigations of abuse or neglect, whenever possible. A child's confidential records should be shared with parents under the guidance of the LSCB.

Children must be supervised at all times and the needs of individual children met. At least one adult must be present in each room or area, indoors and outdoors, while children are using them and two or more staff present in the setting at all times. Staff absences and emergencies must be dealt with through calling in supply staff or asking part-time staff to work extra or different hours, to ensure that children experience a consistent level of care and play experiences.

Staff qualifications and skills

The manager or supervisor and at least half of the other staff must be qualified to level 3 and unqualified staff should be receiving training and working towards at least a level 2 qualification. Many early years practitioners now have further qualifications, such as Early Years Professional or Early Years Teacher status or a degree in early years. A setting should aim to employ one or more of these highly qualified practitioners if possible and also to seek to enhance the qualifications of all staff, by supporting them to continue to undertake appropriate courses, certificates, diplomas and degrees while they are employed.

Having staff of different ages from different backgrounds can be very successful. Employing a fully qualified team is excellent, but recruiting staff who are all young and newly qualified, with little experience, is not always best practice. Managers and senior staff should have several years of experience in a variety of settings and situations. Mature staff, especially those who are parents themselves, who wish to make a career change and are willing to train in the childcare and education profession, can bring invaluable skills to the team alongside qualified and experienced practitioners.

All members of the staff team must have excellent time management skills, being punctual and reliable and completing preparation work when necessary, whatever other commitments and dependents they may have outside the setting. They should demonstrate empathy and understanding for the children and their parents and families and support each other in developing a range of complementary skills to provide a quality childcare environment.

Regular staff meetings should be arranged, at which the team comes together to discuss their practice and to input ideas, knowledge and recent experiences. The manager must ensure that everyone is listened to, initiative is encouraged, ideas are supported and advice is given and accepted fairly and constructively, without criticism. Staff should be given information and training so that they may feel empowered to continuously improve their working practice and develop essential life skills. Self-evaluation may be encouraged for individuals and for the team. There should be a fully understood and agreed commitment to prevent any kind of discrimination from entering the setting, including between staff members, and any confrontations must be aired outside the children's session times.

All adults working in an early years setting should feel able to ask each other for help, support or advice at any time. While each key person must take responsibility for the needs of their own key children, paired and shared keyworking can enhance the children's experiences and improve the quality of adult and child interactions; for example when a key person and buddy worker discuss each child's progress and use their observations to inform the planning of appropriate next steps. Other members of the team may also have useful ideas or advice, especially if they have worked with similar children, families or situations in the past.

Planning and leadership of activities and all essential tasks should be fairly shared out amongst staff members, taking into account that each person may have extra skills or experience in particular areas. All members of the team should take turns to organise snack times, read stories to the group and spend time outside with the children, as well as sharing out duties such as cleaning the children's bathroom and giving out paintings.

But it may be appropriate for one or two particular staff members to lead group singing, dance or drama sessions, while others provide extra art and craft activities and still others offer baking and cookery experiences. Demonstrating and sharing skills is an important part of building an effective team who can offer the best environment and experiences to children.

Adults in the setting must respect each other as individuals and be good role models whenever children are present. They must speak politely to each other and listen to what other people say. When one or two members of staff are leading a whole group activity, others must be joining in and supporting them fully, through setting a good example of listening carefully, demonstrating how to do what is being suggested and managing and controlling the behaviour of children around them to minimise any possible disruptions or distractions.

Children will not remember or follow safety or behavioural rules, such as walking carefully indoors or washing their hands before eating, if they see an adult break these rules. Practitioners must always display behaviour that a child may copy and remind each other of the need for this. Any concerns or disagreements must be talked over and methods or behaviours that other staff members question must be fully discussed, when the children are not present. In order to be a fully effective team, staff must always present a united and consistent set of expectations to children and parents and show that they can all get on in a friendly and caring manner throughout every session.

Effective practice

To make the setting a truly supportive environment, each staff member must regularly evaluate the effectiveness of his or her own practice. Observation skills must be used to provide opportunities for reflective practice, allowing the practitioner to develop greater intuition, identify strengths and weaknesses, avoid repeating mistakes and respect the developing skills of other staff.

To ensure that their practice is effective, practitioners may observe a child and then consider their intended next actions, plan and prepare thoroughly, imagine and visualise the experience to come, then use intuition when setting up the planned learning activity and while engaged in it with the children. They will also use intuition and experience when joining in with children's spontaneous play or offering creative play opportunities based upon the children's ideas or requests.

When an activity or project is finished, it is good and effective practice to analyse what happened, what went well and not so well, whether the learning objective was achieved and whether anything should be done differently if the activity was to be repeated. It may be possible to research other methods and to build the learning gained into future planning.

If parents want to talk, because they have concerns about their children or need more information or support, practitioners must always make time to listen to them. Some parents will ask for an appointment, some prefer to chat before or after a session and some will suddenly find the courage to walk in and admit that they are worried, upset or angry. A setting manager or key person must be available to all of these parents and advise them to the best of their knowledge and ability, making no judgements or assumptions about the family, but drawing on their years of experience in working with other families who may have faced similar situations. If a key person thinks that colleagues may know the answer to a question or have more experience in a particular area, he or she could consider suggesting to the parent that they could be invited to join them to discuss the matter, but should make it clear that this is optional and respect whatever the parent decides.

Parents whose children are diagnosed with a special or additional need, disability, medical condition or behavioural disorder will need a great deal of support to come to terms with this, and will also need help to work with other professionals to get the best treatment or advice for their child. Early years practitioners must make it clear to them that they and their child are extremely valued and wanted within their early years setting and that they are welcome to ask for help or come in to talk at any time. Setting staff must always work with other health professionals and therapists to implement a consistent programme for a child and make sure that what they do complements what parents do at home.

When children are due to move to another setting, it is important to offer support appropriate to the situation, which may be accompanying them on visits to the local primary school reception class or ensuring files are up to date, discussed and handed to parents to take with them when they leave the area or the country.

Practitioners should always encourage children to make friends and play with each other, identifying children who have similar interests and play preferences and providing opportunities for them to choose to be together, as well as praising all children for participating in activities co-operatively with others. Adjusting activities and offering them on various levels can accommodate the learning styles of children with delayed development. Identifying children whose level of development is considerably higher than average and encouraging them to work and play together when appropriate may provide extra challenges to ensure that they do not become bored and unhappy or disruptive.

Early years practitioners have the interesting and challenging but rewarding task of explaining how children learn, what levels and stages each child has reached, whether these fall within the range of development usually expected for a child of that age, which opportunities will be offered to the children and how parents can continue to be a vital part of their child's learning journey. Each family must be monitored sensitively to ensure that they receive all the support and praise that they need, until their child moves on to the next stage of their care and education. Working as a team, colleagues must strive always

Making the setting a safe and supportive environment

Figure 4.4 Offer new challenges to enable more confident or experienced children to work together and maintain enthusiasm for activities.

to support, respect and encourage each other, to share skills and experiences and to make every early years setting a happy, welcoming and supportive environment for its children and families.

Understanding and promoting children's development

Children's interests should initiate and vary the themes offered within an early years setting and staff should plan flexibly to accommodate new ideas and developments as they arise. The practitioners' role is to provide for the children of their setting a safe, secure and stimulating environment and to promote their development through offering enjoyable activities based on their interests, knowing that they learn and develop most easily when absorbed in self-chosen play. Therefore, it is important to strive to provide achievable challenges, the right degree of risk and new ideas for play, so that children may develop as they wish.

> A four-year-old visited a castle with her family and continued to talk about castles for days after returning to her pre-school. Other children quickly began to show an interest in castles too. This provided a good opportunity for her key person and colleagues to develop a new theme led by the children's ideas. Adults and children enthusiastically painted large cardboard castle walls together and created a new role play area. They made shields and armour, crowns and princess hats for dressing up, collected and shared songs, stories and non-fiction books about castles and discussed the types of food that people in castles would have eaten and the animals they might have kept.

Practitioners need to listen to all children in the setting and be aware of what interests and inspires them. They need to plan themes and activities flexibly and be willing to accommodate extra ideas or change direction in order to

Understanding and promoting children's development

encourage children to develop their own passions. They also need to have open-ended resources, such as art and craft materials, books, CDs and the internet, available at all times so that they may respond to anything that a child wants to make or find out more about.

> A three-year-old developed a passion for making rockets, from craft materials and construction kits indoors and from planks and tyres in the garden. He talked about them to his key person and his peers and displayed a great deal of knowledge about space travel. Led by his key person, practitioners at his nursery provided books, small world figures, music, games and puzzles on a space theme and helped the children to make spaceships, helmets, oxygen tanks and planets from recycled materials, so that they could dress up as astronauts and engage in imaginative role play or act out stories.

Every early years setting must have a collection of good books on a variety of themes, including both fiction and non-fiction titles, so that children may discover more about any interest that they have. Practitioners will find that many themes are popular with all children aged two to five years and so the same books will be useful year after year, with each new intake of children, although they may be explored at different times and in different orders. Different ones can be purchased and added gradually, when a child suggests a new interest to be investigated.

Small world people and animal figures may be used to create any situations, along with wooden or plastic bricks and other construction kits. It may be worth investing in some more specific kits which are always popular and provide valuable play and learning opportunities, such as farm, police, fire and hospital characters, vehicles and accessories, but practitioners should play alongside children to demonstrate how any item can be used symbolically to create a satisfying imaginative game.

Providing for all areas of learning

All areas of learning should be developed, by offering equipment and activities such as books, puzzles, games, malleable materials, sand, water, mark

Understanding and promoting children's development

Figure 5.1 Children can use small world figures to create satisfying imaginative games.

making, arts and crafts, role play, construction toys, small world play, computers, musical instuments and music sources, large fixed play equipment, wheeled vehicles, balls, beanbags, hoops, buckets, tyres, planks, crates and boxes, trampolines, and parachutes. Recycled and found materials should be collected for modelling and collage work, natural resources used in the outdoor area, loose parts available throughout the setting, indoors and outside, and the moving of equipment between different areas should be encouraged to facilitate absorbing, creative and imaginative play.

An example of constructive, high quality planning, including each of the prime and specific areas of learning and development, for three- to five-year-old children within an early years setting might include the following.

1. Creating puppet shows (Personal, Social and Emotional Development)

To enable children to interact with each other and with adults; to explore and express ideas and feelings; to develop independence skills and begin to understand teamwork; to help and encourage each other to use a wider vocabulary; and to remember the sequences of popular stories, discuss well-known characters and imagine how they might speak, behave and feel.

For some children, this will be a new experience that introduces them to traditional stories and characters and encourages the early development of thinking, imagining and discussion skills. Others will be familiar with some stories and ready to act them out with puppets, learning to work together co-operatively and give voices to characters.

More able children will naturally take the lead in directing other children to create a whole show, as they are confident in remembering stories and ready to practise leadership, using advanced social and people management skills. Children with particular special needs, such as behavioural, emotional or social difficulties, may learn more about how to predict, understand or empathise with the feelings and reactions of others through this activity.

2. Listening to stories, joining in with repeated phrases and chants, answering questions and discussing events, characters and feelings (Communication and Language)

To encourage all children to feel included; to develop good listening skills and the ability to speak out appropriately within a smaller or larger group of familiar people, while experiencing a range of writing styles, rich vocabulary, dialogue, rhymes and alliteration.

Some children will be learning how to sit and listen and take in information and ideas from a leading adult and other children around them. Others will respond to the enthusiasm of the group and be able to anticipate repeated phrases or chants, remember story sequences and supply missing words or answers to simple questions.

Children with more advanced skills will be able to describe characters or events in more detail, respond to more complicated questions and offer ideas, opinions and experiences of their own. Children with special educational needs or English as an additional language will benefit from hearing spoken English in conjunction with illustrations and a clear storyline and should quickly learn to join in with some repeated phrases and chants, which will aid their thinking and pronunciation skills.

3. Playing outdoors with large play equipment, such as a tunnel, bridge and climbing frame, or planks, crates, tyres and barrels (Physical Development)

To enable children to attempt and practise new and existing skills in climbing, balancing, swinging and jumping, gaining confidence in using their own

Understanding and promoting children's development

bodies to move in a variety of ways and experiencing the positive benefits of being active outside, while involving themselves in close social interactions with their peers, as they climb and balance together and around each other, showing care and concern for others to keep everybody safe, which promotes a sense of well-being.

Some children will ask an adult to provide support and remain close by while they nervously attempt new skills, such as walking across a beam or jumping from a step. Others will negotiate the equipment confidently and may accept suggestions for new challenges, as they begin to gain the confidence to include manageable risks in their play.

More experienced children will devise ever greater challenges for themselves, which they may attempt in co-operation with others, and may also choose to help and teach less confident children new skills. Children with physical or learning disabilities may need one-to-one support from caring adults in order to devise and meet challenges in small, manageable steps, to enable them to experience the satisfaction of achievement and gradually develop a greater self-confidence.

4. Drawing pictures of favourite story characters and making up stories and scenarios involving the characters (Literacy)

To encourage children to make their own marks, choosing colours and giving meaning to the marks that they make, as they attempt to create representational drawings of characters; and to describe them and their adventures through emergent writing and early letter formation, with the support of adults when they request it.

Some children will hold tools with a palmar grasp and explore the movements that they can make with a pencil, pen, crayon, chalk or paintbrush, without trying to create a specific end result. Others will be experimenting with different grips and combining tools and colours to create imaginative patterns and symbols, possibly including a series of marks that look like writing or some letters of their own names.

Children with highly developed skills will use a pincer or tripod grip and manipulate tools with increasing control to create recognisable pictures and representations, which they can name and describe and may write using recognisable letters and attempts at spelling words based on their knowledge of phonic sounds. With the right level of support, encouragement and supervision, children with special needs may explore making marks with a variety of tools and resources and begin to express their own ideas.

5. Making a house in the role play area, for the three bears or the seven dwarfs, with toy food, plates, cups, bowls, spoons, blankets and soft toys (Mathematics)

To allow children to recreate the situations they have encountered in the traditional stories; to decide what is needed and work out how to achieve it using the resources available; to solve their own problems and draw their own conclusions with counting, reasoning, thinking logically and sharing skills and ideas.

Some children will be able to match plates and bowls to soft toys, count some of them and demonstrate practically how to share out resources amongst a small group. Others will describe sizes and shapes, count, add and take away.

Very able children will predict, estimate and discuss what they will need to recreate specific situations from stories and may use a range of props, begin to include concepts of time and space in their play and choose to draw and write shapes and numerals to describe and enhance their ideas. Children with special needs may begin to learn about one-to-one correspondence or gain some understanding of how or why certain items may be symbolically linked to particular characters.

6. Floating and sinking experiments in the water tray (Understanding the World)

To offer children opportunities to handle different materials; to learn new vocabulary; to understand the words 'floating' and 'sinking' as they are explained, demonstrated and used by a supportive adult; to develop their curiosity and logical thinking through practical activity; to sustain interest for extended periods; and to share their surprises and satisfactions with others.

Some children will work alone with an adult and choose the directions in which to take their own learning, discovering which objects float or sink and gradually beginning to use those words, as well as more practical explanations of what is happening. Others will work in pairs, stimulating each other to

Understanding and promoting children's development

guess and then try out different objects, sharing ideas of why some float and some sink and recording their findings with pictures or stickers.

More mature children will be able to manage working in groups of three or four, taking turns to make predictions and to offer explanations for why they were right or wrong, discussing known facts and surprises co-operatively and recording results in a range of ways. Water is both soothing and stimulating for children with physical or learning disabilities or sensory impairments. They may be encouraged to use their most developed skills and senses to explore objects and to record how water affects them as an introduction to new ideas and learning experiences which can be offered gradually.

7. *Making models for display from craft resources and recycled and found materials (Expressive Arts and Design)*

To encourage children to choose from a range of pieces and joining materials and learn about their properties and which are most effectively used together, becoming absorbed in self-selected tasks and projects and working alone or collaborating with peers, with the support of an adult when necessary to prevent frustration or abandonment of an idea before it is fully explored.

Some children will explore resources and equipment, such as pens, glues, boxes, tubes and collage pieces, and ask for adult help if they cannot achieve their ideas alone. Others will practise skills, such as drawing, cutting out and joining pieces with sticky tape, and appreciate talking to adults about their models, knowing that their work is valued.

Especially creative children will be ready to take risks and create more imaginative and ambitious designs, while others will wish to make detailed representations of real items and produce logical or symbolic creations that are instantly recognisable. Children with special needs must be encouraged to offer their own creative ideas and be supported in achieving them. Adults may need to complete a great deal of the work themselves in some cases, but the children should be involved and consulted at every stage and praised for every effort and contribution.

In all areas, adults may extend children's learning and add to their enjoyment by joining in with games; providing further equipment as appropriate, such as magnifying glasses, pieces of fabric, spades or sticks; or leading ring games, dancing, drama, songs, rhymes and stories. Practitioners and parents may strengthen relationships by sharing children's interests and achievements, games and ideas, comments, artwork and models with each other and through working as partners in care and learning.

Encouraging more independence

As soon as they are ready, individual children should be supported in gradually learning to use the toilet independently, to dress and undress themselves, to change their own shoes and to decide when they need to wear coats, hats and gloves. They should understand the importance of eating and drinking healthily and how to make some good choices, as well as eating, drinking and serving themselves with decreasing adult support, and sharing meals and snacks sociably. They also need to know about good hygiene practices, such as when and how to wash their hands.

Children should be encouraged to play for extended periods of time, so that they may become absorbed in their chosen activities and follow their own interests and particular schemas, indoors or outdoors, before they are asked to tidy up together and participate in a whole group activity, such as a story or discussion, songs and rhymes, acting and drama, a puppet show or a game. Both individual play and small group play are valuable, and opportunities to practise co-operation and teamwork as a member of a larger group are also important.

A plan which brings together the ideas and decisions of all practitioners within a setting's staff team ensures that there are links to all areas of the curriculum and makes it easy for each key person to carry out observations of particular activities at set times, as well as less formal, spontaneous ones, and to record their children's progress and achievements in their profiles. Any areas of concern can then also be seen and monitored easily from their earliest stages.

Children have the right to be kept safe, helped to thrive and supported to fulfil their potential. However, this does not mean excluding all risks and challenges from their lives. Children should be encouraged to learn to take and manage reasonable risks and to engage in challenging play, accepting that minor accidents and failures will occasionally happen. They need opportunities to enjoy messy play and to try new foods, ideas and experiences. They will only acquire new skills and make progress if they are encouraged to try things out, make their own connections, stretch themselves and reach for the stars.

Understanding and promoting children's development

Figure 5.2 An adult's active involvement can allow children of different ages to participate safely and constructively in activities together.

Early years settings must meet the legal requirements and follow the guidelines of the Statutory Framework for the Early Years Foundation Stage to provide a good and appropriate experience for every child, from which they can make the most of their abilities and talents as they grow up. Activities should always be accessible to children at various levels, offering enough challenge to the highest achievers, but enough interest to younger or less experienced children or those with special or additional needs. This may require an adult to be actively involved in some activities at certain times or when particular children wish to participate.

Sometimes, children prefer to play alone or with close friends and it is more appropriate for adults to provide general supervision, without interfering in the play, but making themselves available when needed. Adults should be aware that they can unconsciously take over, redirect or change children's play, through joining in or asking too many questions, and that this is not a good thing, as sometimes valuable independent learning can be lost.

Differentiation within the curriculum

To stimulate very able, gifted and talented children, practitioners can pose challenging questions, suggest ways to adapt or add to games or resources and praise and encourage creative thinking and positive social interactions. Children with differing abilities or less experience may benefit from one-to-one support; specifically prepared or adapted resources; different approaches to games; or more time or repetition to extend their learning.

Differentiation within the curriculum is important because practitioners must recognise and understand each child as an individual and provide activities that meet all children's needs, allowing them to explore and express their differences. A differentiated curriculum will include open-ended play and learning activities that may be accessed by all children and developed as they wish, allowing enjoyment at all levels, from the simple play of the youngest children and those with special needs to the extra challenges added by the oldest or most able. This is vital to prevent frustration, which could cause children to withdraw from play and exploration and be unhappy; or boredom, which often leads to undesirable behaviour or a child stultifying at a particular stage or level. Such lack of motivation does not promote learning or development in any child.

The information in each child's profile, which practitioners share with each other during sessions and at staff meetings, can be used to plan how to meet the diverse learning needs of the group. It may be obvious that some children enjoy boisterous play while others prefer quiet activities, and that some are happy to play independently within an established group of friends while others are still at the solitary or parallel play stage or need more adult support. Some children will choose to go outside for a significant part of the session every day, but others may demonstrate their preference to stay indoors for much of the time.

Whenever possible, activities should be offered both indoors and outdoors and on larger and smaller scales, to suit the preferred learning styles of all children. Role play, construction toys, sand and water, beanbags and buckets, books, drawing, dolls and science experiments can be provided both indoors and outdoors. Children who prefer to be outside can be encouraged to sometimes take part in craft activities and games or use a computer indoors. Those who like to be inside can often be enticed out by the inclusion of tricycles and scooters, footballs or climbing frames in the provision. Alternatively, they could just take their favourite play materials with them when moving between the two areas.

Any children currently following schemas should be able to find many opportunities to do so within their play. They may wish to transport objects, position them carefully or turn them or themselves upside down. Vertical,

Understanding and promoting children's development

Figure 5.3 Offer favourite toys, such as tricycles and scooters, to encourage children who are reluctant to play outside.

horizontal and later diagonal lines and movements may be explored, or the throwing of things through the air, along with large arm and leg movements. Children may wish to enclose or envelop objects or themselves, using bricks, boxes, paper or blankets. They may be absorbed by things that turn and roll, or by materials that change, or by ordering or connecting pieces. Their drawings may show circles, radials or one-to-one correspondence. They may begin to understand how one function depends upon another.

Brain research has shown that learning takes place due to neurons in the brain making connections and allowing information to flow across synapses. When synapses are not used, they fade away, but, if used repeatedly, they make strong, permanent connections. We know from this that children need lots of opportunities to repeat and practise skills and to relate their learning to previous experiences. For example, having familiar books and posters or friezes on display for a prolonged period allows children to return to them as often as they wish and to ask questions or repeat sounds, words or sentences until they feel confident enough to use them in their daily lives.

There are many articles available online that describe the findings of brain research relating to the development of young children, many of them from the USA. Some areas that might be of interest to early years practitioners working with families and communities are:

- 'Baby's brain begins now' (The Urban Child Institute, 2015)
- 'Brain anatomy and brain development timeline' (Better Brains for Babies, 2015)
- 'Brain development research can influence early childhood curriculum' (Colbert, *Early Childhood News*, 2008)
- 'Early brain development research, review and update' (Schiller, *Child Care Exchange*, 2010)

There are numerous other online sites and articles that may also be helpful.

Allowing children to make choices

Children should be involved in making decisions and choices regarding the issues which affect them directly. A setting may offer a selection of play resources and activities, from which children can freely choose, and allow children to decide for themselves where and with whom they would like to play. For example, if they choose to involve themselves in a craft project, they should make the decisions as to which resources and equipment they will use and in which direction they will take their project.

Understanding and promoting children's development

An open snack time arrangement, such as a café system, encourages children to decide for themselves when they are hungry or thirsty, and then, when they come to the dining area, to choose what and how much to eat, from what is on offer. They may also choose where they would like to sit and, perhaps, who to sit with, although this may require some negotiation when many children are choosing, as their choices may not match!

Older children need increasing amounts of freedom to make their own choices and decisions as they mature. Children aged between three and five years appreciate adults who listen to them and concentrate on what they say, allowing them to express opinions and contribute ideas. If such relationships are well established, they can often be encouraged to negotiate and reach an amicable decision when they disagree with each other or with adults. They start to choose their own friends and activities from this age and these gradually become more important to them. They become more independent, can understand explanations to help them to make appropriate choices and can begin to take responsibility for some of their decisions. They continue to explore their own identities and develop their own personalities.

Children continuously make choices about what to do, what to think and how to behave, but they also need to make decisions on how to fit in with different people and in different situations, adapting their behaviour to suit their lives at home, at school, in clubs, with strangers, with family members and with friends.

When working with children at any stage of development, adults should ask appropriate open-ended questions and encourage debates, avoiding questions with only yes/no answers or only one correct answer and ensuring that they do not lead children by displaying biased opinions of their own. Children have choices when they are able to select from a variety of resources or ideas, offered freely in an inclusive environment, and exercise the power of choosing that is their right. They may then often be able to come to a decision that settles an issue, reaches a conclusion or makes a resolve.

If children are encouraged to make some choices from a very young age, they are more likely to become co-operative and learn the essential skill of negotiation. As they grow older, more and more independent choices will gradually become appropriate, and, if they are encouraged to practise choosing, they will become better at it until mostly sensible choices will be made and respectful relationships with parents, siblings and teachers can be maintained. For example, toddlers may be asked which of two t-shirts they choose to wear, while four-year-olds might be trusted to select

Understanding and promoting children's development

Figure 5.4 Children are able to adapt their activities, choices and behaviours when they wish to play with family members or friends.

from the cupboard, choosing old clothes for the garden but smarter ones for an outing.

Many decisions can be taken by children as they grow up. Sometimes they might decide wrongly, but this can be a valuable learning experience and should be allowed to happen if the consequences will not be serious. Deciding not to wear gloves on a cold day, using weak glue to stick heavy materials together or allowing an unreliable friend to borrow something quickly prove themselves to be bad decisions, but children will learn more effectively if they can remember suffering discomfort or frustration and thus make a different decision next time. However, all choices and decisions must be monitored by adults and, if necessary, refused in order to keep a young child safe. For example, it is essential to explain exactly why we must never touch the oven, jump from the top of the stairs or walk into a busy road and then accept no further discussion on such matters.

Within an early years setting, or any group or club to which children belong, it is important to involve them in making choices about the way they would most like to work and play and the equipment and activities they would like to have on offer, as well as decisions as to what should happen to anyone who spoils things for the others and what rules there should be to keep things fair for everybody. If they feel that they have made the rules themselves, they will be much more likely to abide by them and, if they have participated in choosing toys and equipment, they will usually take better care of them. Group rules should be suitably worded and explained so that young children can understand what they mean, but should always include the need to respect each individual and to value the diversity of the people who belong to the setting or club.

Making observations

Through making regular detailed observations of each child, practitioners can use the information gathered to check and assess children's progress, especially when they are struggling in an area, practising hard to acquire a new skill or demonstrating a new level of ability or confidence. They will then be able to decide when to provide opportunities for more repetition, or different ways to apply and practise a new skill, and when and in what direction to move on and plan for a new target or next step. In this way, they can be sure of meeting each child's needs.

Observations of individual children allow practitioners to understand their needs, abilities and preferences and to find out exactly what stage each child is at and how this affects their interactions with others. Assessments based on observations enable practitioners to identify areas of development in which children are advanced or delayed, secure or lacking in confidence, needing encouragement or looking for extra challenges.

Experienced practitioners with detailed knowledge of children and their developmental stages will recognise types of behaviour seen during observations and understand what causes children to act and react in certain ways. They will use this understanding and assessment to plan activities, resources and play experiences to meet their children's needs, taking into account any schemas or particular interests, within a curriculum appropriate for all children in the group.

Observation and assessment also provide the necessary evidence to allow practitioners to make referrals to other professionals or consult with them, and to talk to parents, support them and work with them, to improve outcomes for children with individual needs at different stages of their lives. They are a vital part of ensuring that diverse individual needs are being met and that the staff of a setting are making their practice truly inclusive for all children and families.

> Several observations of a three-year-old boy showed that he was very interested in covering things up. On one occasion, he wrapped a large piece of playdough in sheets of paper and left it on the window sill. The following day, he covered the dolls with blankets and put them into bed, then later he buried the toy dinosaurs in the sand. His key person identified that he was following an enclosing and enveloping schema and provided other resources to encourage his learning through this interest. She invited him to create letters inside envelopes in the mark-making area, to make dens with swathes of fabric and to enjoy role play in a packaging factory, with wrapping papers, scissors, sticky tape and boxes.

Effective observation allows practitioners to identify each particular interest and schema followed by each of their key children as they occur. They may then use their professional knowledge and experience, along with the equipment and resources that they have available within the setting, to plan a variety of ways in which to develop these. Children are more likely to achieve appropriate next steps and make good progress in all areas of learning if they are encouraged to follow their own enthusiasms.

Being aware of theory and research

In order to understand the interplay between theory and practice, practitioners need to regularly update their knowledge on current research and the reasons for it being undertaken. Reading professional magazines or information on websites can aid in this. It is wise to also be aware of new books published in areas relevant to the job role and setting, and to buy or borrow them for the staff team when possible, so that they may read and discuss them to evaluate the research and conclusions they include.

Before believing each new theory presented in a book, report or article, practitioners must check whether enough research has been done and how far it proves or disproves the theory. It is necessary to check whether the facts and information are reliable and whether they can be usefully applied within a setting and a practitioner's role. Some researchers may not have interpreted

Understanding and promoting children's development

data entirely without bias or their own opinions, or may have tried too hard to make the research prove a theory, thereby losing some vital objectivity. Different theories are popular at different times and being influenced by these fashions and trends can affect or prevent truly objective research. Applying theory to practice ensures that practitioners know both what to do and why they must do it, enabling them to contribute significantly and effectively to the progress and development of every child.

Planning for learning

Practitioners benefit from clear planning and learning objectives, as these can make them feel more confident and positive about their work each day and avoid any wasted time or conflict of interests between staff when preparing the learning environment and resources. It is possible to see immediately from a clearly written plan if any area of development is under-represented and if there are ample opportunities for visual, auditory and kinaesthetic learners to play and explore.

Planning ahead ensures that resources do not run out before they are needed and staff do not duplicate ideas. Provision can be made within the curriculum to meet all individual needs that have been identified and all opportunities can be offered in a non-discriminatory way. All children must feel that their play is valued and any attempts to stereotype or prevent access due to gender, race, disability or any other bias must be challenged and prevented.

Colleagues may discuss and review the progress of individual children between themselves and with a manager, using profiles as evidence, especially if they have concerns that a child will not meet enough of the early learning goals within the time expected, or if they have identified a child of exceptionally high ability or with specific learning needs. When targets for individual children are identified, they should be promoted through activities which are appropriate to each child's interests and preferred learning styles and which offer achievable challenges. Observation and assessment can be very effective in meeting individual children's needs, but only when used correctly by experienced practitioners and not if used in isolation and never checked or backed up by information obtained from other sources.

It is useful to make comparisons with the normative stages of development that all children pass through, to allow a child's individual progress to be monitored and extra support offered if any developmental delay or very high ability is identified. But it is important not to compare children with each other, as all children develop at their own individual rates and in different areas at different times. Inclusive practice values this diversity and encourages children to be themselves.

It is a practitioner's professional responsibility to consider each child when planning, taking into account the wide range of individual needs and abilities and different learning styles of the children within the group. When children believe that the adults at their setting will provide suitable and enjoyable activities for them at each session, and feel secure in warm and caring relationships based on mutual respect, they will be settled, happy, confident, and able and willing to learn and achieve.

Recording children's progress and achievements

A profile is a record of a child's progress, achievements, individual needs and interests, and is often called a learning journey. It will usually be kept by a child's key person within an early years setting. The person responsible for keeping a child's profile invites contributions from other staff within the setting, as well as from the child, parents, other family members and other carers.

When a child moves on to school, a teacher or teaching assistant within the reception or foundation class, as well as a member of staff in any after-school club or holiday-care setting, will also be required to observe, record, monitor and assess progress in this way until the child leaves the Early Years Foundation Stage (EYFS) and begins the National Curriculum in primary school, at the beginning of Year One.

Observations and assessments

In her book, *How To Observe Children*, Sheila Riddall-Leech explains why observing and assessing children is important:

> One of the fundamental purposes of observing children is to enable adults to gain greater understanding of their needs. All children have unique qualities. If we are to meet children's individual needs effectively it is essential that we recognise their differences and acknowledge that they have a right to be treated with respect.
>
> (2008: 1)

Using a mixture of different observation and assessment techniques, and sharing information as a staff team, allows practitioners to build a relevant and detailed profile for each individual child. However, some assessments can be short and written in a style that does not provide enough information to reliably meet all of a child's individual needs. Observations may be affected by a number of factors and will not always give a true picture of a child's abilities or needs, leading, at times, to incomplete or incorrect assessments being made. If practitioners are not yet very knowledgeable about the children in their care, or not experienced in carrying out observations and assessments, the wrong conclusions may sometimes be drawn or important information may be missed. For these reasons, less experienced practitioners should continue to receive guidance and support from a mentor until they are confident in their roles.

When observing children, practitioners must remain objective and report exactly what they see and hear, honestly and accurately. They must not rely on previous knowledge of a child or make assumptions and must never allow their own opinions, feelings or values to alter the information gained or to influence the way it is recorded.

Observation and assessment have an important role to play in the building of profiles of individual children. A specific observation can be evidence or proof that a child has acquired a new skill, or is still developing one and needs more practice and support. It can identify a child's interests and preferences or areas of greater or lesser knowledge and understanding.

An assessment of children's levels of development in any of the areas of learning uses direct observations to inform practitioners of whether the children are achieving within the expected level for their age group, or demonstrating advanced skills or developmental delay.

Formal and informal observations of children allow staff to know and understand them thoroughly, to discuss their progress with each other and to make informed assessments.

This is one of the most reliable ways of gathering information and provides a major contribution towards the building of children's individual profiles. These profiles establish developmental stages and levels, measure progress and inform planning. The themes and activities planned should always be offered inclusively, so that they can be accessed by all children as individuals.

A file should be created for each child, which groups long and short observations into the seven areas of learning and development and also includes other relevant information, such as progress notes and suggested next steps, which will be reviewed and re-set approximately each half-term or every six to eight weeks, along with photographs, comments and contributions

Recording children's progress and achievements

Figure 6.1 Create a file for each child, including observations, progress, photographs, examples and next steps.

from parents and carers, examples of children's artwork, drawing and writing and reports by other professionals working with the child or family.

However, observations do not always give a true picture of a child, as other factors can influence findings on any particular day. Some activities can be limited by weather conditions, a piece of equipment not working or resources running out. Sometimes children may react differently when best friends are absent or when they are trying to offer support to a new or younger child. The play and learning of the children being observed may, at times, be disrupted by the undesirable behaviour of other children and this can influence their responses and make them leave a game quickly or become frustrated while participating in an activity.

It is important that practitioners assess findings carefully and repeat an observation if conclusions are not clear, avoiding deciding that a child has or has not achieved a particular skill or maturity level before they are completely sure. If they see children zipping up their own coats and putting on outdoor shoes unaided, they know that this skill has been acquired, but, if children ask for help without trying alone, further observation and support will be needed, as they may actually be able to manage independently but are just feeling tired or less confident today. Sometimes, children may be very close to achieving a skill and ready to master it, but only if they receive the right type of support and encouragement at the perfect moment.

If parents state that their children can write their own name at home but they never name their own drawings in the setting, despite enough opportunity and encouragement to do so, a note should be included from the parent within the child's profile and then more observations made in the mark-making area over a period of time. It can sometimes be up to six weeks before a child feels confident enough to display a skill already acquired at home within their early years setting.

Involving families

Observation and assessment alone is not the most effective way of knowing individual children and understanding how to meet all of their needs. It is vital to form good relationships with children's parents, families and all other carers, engaging in constructive conversations with them in order to gather more information. Many children may attend two or more different early years settings each week and all settings attended by an individual child must liaise and share information with each other, to ensure that a full and accurate picture of the child can be built and their needs consistently met, wherever they are.

Early years practitioners should talk with parents and show the profile to them often, sharing recent observations, particular achievements, new interests and amusing episodes. They will sometimes find that they can then add a note to a child's profile stating that the parent has also seen the child do this outside the setting, or that the parent is now encouraged to provide a popular toy or book or offer stimulating resources or activities at home.

If a child's primary carer is another relative, or a nanny or childminder, they will also like to share the profile with the key person and may have observations, pictures and comments of their own to add. Celebrating new achievements with children and their carers is very rewarding. Children need to feel sure that all of the adults in their lives are working together consistently and they love to hear their achievements being shared, because it often means double the praise!

Practitioners may report that a child has learned to pedal or hop, to build up a tower of six bricks, to recognise or write their own name, or to fasten the buttons of their coat without help. Parents may tell of important events and experiences, good or bad, that may affect their child's progress or well-being,

Recording children's progress and achievements

Figure 6.2 Carers should spend quality time together to share observations, celebrate achievements and strengthen relationships, for the benefit of each individual child.

such as play and relationships with older siblings, cousins and friends; new babies or pets or cars; family illness or bereavement; or moving house. They may report on achievements that can only be seen outside the setting, such as swimming, dance, drama, gym, sport or music lessons; leading to certificates, exams or participation in events, performances or matches.

Parents should know that they can look at or add to their own child's profile at any time. The setting may provide special sheets for this purpose or just invite them to make contributions in any way they choose. Parents may prefer to write accounts or comments, or to supply photographs or copies of certificates. Written submissions may be in the family's first language if this is not English, as the profile will eventually be theirs to keep, but it may be possible for somebody to also supply an English translation, or to explain verbally what has been written, for the benefit of setting staff and the Office for Standards in Education (Ofsted) inspectors who do not speak that language.

In some cases, practitioners may find it appropriate to offer to write the information themselves but then ask parents to read, consider, check and amend it before its inclusion in the profile. It is important to be sensitive to the needs of parents as individuals. Some will be highly literate and wish to contribute to their child's profile independently. Others may be less confident, have poor literacy skills, English as an additional language or a disability, and prefer to receive help from the key person.

Recording children's progress and achievements

A profile should include some examples of the child's artwork and creativity, such as drawings and paintings, and photographs of larger pieces, 3D models, masks and works-in-progress. Practitioners can also add other projects, such as attempts to write their name or other letters or numbers; matching and sorting activities; charts on which the child has recorded data; and pieces of careful cutting out. This is especially appropriate if several examples are available which demonstrate significant progress in skills, imagination and creativity. Parents can be encouraged to bring in examples too. They may like to safely keep their child's best pictures and early writing in this way, and be able to take photographs of models made from recycled materials or construction kits at home before they are broken up.

Photographs of constructive, imaginative and physical play, such as play-dough shapes and patterns, dressing up, role play or riding a scooter, should appear throughout the profile, often accompanying or illustrating specific observations or new stepping stones and early learning goals achieved.

Next steps

At approximately six to ten week intervals, or once a school term or half-term, each key person will decide on some next steps for each of their key children. They may discuss these with the other practitioners within the setting to check their suitability and appropriate levels. When children first join a setting, each key person will spend a short period of time getting to know the children and observing what they can do already and what they are trying to do next. It will then be possible to set some next steps based on the children's current interests, which will encourage them to make progress in important areas. A committed and experienced key person will be able to monitor children's progress as they engage in free and spontaneous play and to offer support, make suggestions, extend learning and add resources as appropriate.

Practitioners can target particular children to be included in some activities, in order to see whether progress has been made, if a leap has been taken in ability, skills or confidence, or when there is a willingness to try a new or previously disliked activity. They can see if there is cause for concern or an unusual approach or outcome and can then speak to a parent if they are puzzled or need to check a skill or attitude.

If, through observation, practitioners identify areas in which children have made significantly less progress than in others, or issues that are a cause for concern, these will be included in one or more of the next steps. For example, children who are very articulate and can write their own names but cannot put on their own shoes to play in the garden, will need to work on self-care and independence skills before learning to write sentences. Children who can play simple computer games and share out the dominoes beautifully but are not yet toilet trained, will need to work on leaving nappies behind before learning to play ludo.

Children who find it hard to share toys or to wait for their turn for attention can develop these skills gradually if they are set small achievement goals, one after another. If they are prone to tantrums and screaming when they don't have their own way, they may spend a few weeks learning to wait calmly for a minute or two, then a few weeks practising asking politely for their turn, then a few weeks developing the ability to pass toys to other children.

If all staff within the setting are aware of the goals set, they will work consistently to support the children and praise them for their achievements, however small, recording observations of the children attempting or succeeding in the desired skills and behaviours. It will be easy to identify progress made by children in many areas from their profiles, using the next steps planned for them during their terms spent in the early years setting and the observations made by the key person and colleagues.

A pre-school child had the following observations recorded in her profile:

Personal, Social and Emotional Development
From September to December, ES only watched other children and played in parallel or with an adult. By January, she copied what other children were doing, chatted and made models with them. In February and March, ES was observed to select and organise play with toy food in the kitchen role-play area, as a member of a small group, and to dress up and act out fairytales with two friends.

Mathematics
In October, while playing with shapes, ES was able to say the numbers she needed, guess to find them and check by counting. In March, she was observed counting and sorting groups of coloured counters very confidently.

Recording children's progress and achievements

> **Literacy**
> Through November and December, ES was observed making the two middle letters of her name, then adding the first capital and then the last letter. During January, she talked herself through writing the capital first, then each of the three other letters, unaided. By the end of January, she could write her name alone and check it for herself.

Each set of next steps, which will be stepping stones and early learning goals taken from the Statutory Framework for the EYFS, will be detailed in turn and the information drawn from observations recorded alongside them to provide proof that the child is progressing and achieving at a speed and level appropriate to her age and that her key person has no concerns about her skills or development. If any of the next steps are not achieved by the end of the projected period, they may be carried over so that the child will continue to work on them, adapted slightly to allow a greater chance of success, or replaced with more realistic aims.

The key person will decide what is most appropriate, based on knowledge and understanding of the child and possibly discussion with colleagues or a parent or guardian and the child. Practitioners may discuss and review the progress of individual children between themselves or with a manager, using observations and profiles as evidence, especially if they have concerns that a child will not meet early learning goals within the time expected, or if they have identified a child of exceptionally high ability or with specific learning needs.

Next steps should always be shared with parents on a regular basis. Some will prefer a key person to read them out and explain each one, while others will prefer to read them for themselves and then ask about anything they don't understand or agree with. There should be space within a child's profile for parents to comment in writing before signing to indicate that the next steps have been shared with them and that they agree with them. Each key person will review the next steps for each key child before setting new ones and will also write an overview of development for each child, which will be shown to parents, for them to sign if they are happy with it. If there are any issues at this point, they will be discussed and resolved before the parent is asked to sign anything.

The overview for the child previously described would be:

ES is developing and achieving steadily and I am able to identify evidence of progress from her profile. She joined the pre-school aged 3 years, 1 month. At first, she was very quiet and appeared shy. She did not talk to other children or to the adults she did not already know and found her key person whenever she needed help or support. She stood and watched activities, followed her key person around the rooms and had to be encouraged to take part in an activity. Once engaged, she stayed there and needed encouragement and support to move to different play, even when it was obvious that she had finished what she was doing.

Now, at the age of 3 years, 8 months, she chooses activities independently and plays co-operatively with friends. She speaks confidently to all familiar adults and displays skills and competencies in all areas of development. The observations in her profile show much progress and development. Her planned next steps have been achieved, some quickly and some more gradually, over the two terms she has been attending the pre-school.

Parent consultations

Arranging appointments for more formal consultations, two or three times a year, allows parents to look at profiles in detail with practitioners, at pre-arranged quiet and private times. This is an opportunity for either party to share any concerns or to discuss in detail the stages that children have reached in each area of learning and development, what they might achieve next and how this could be encouraged.

When making individual profiles to share with parents and carers, care must be taken to ensure that no confidentiality is breached for other clients. The information shared must be relevant and useful and this may involve detailing the other children most usually played with and some significant interactions. Questions most frequently asked at parent consultations are 'Who does he play with?' and 'Who are her friends?'.

Of course, parents like to know who their child plays with and will speak to other parents about their child's friends and hopefully make friends too. But

Recording children's progress and achievements

Figure 6.3 Parents like to know who their children play with and the types of games, activities and projects they create and enjoy with their friends.

all observations should only include facts about the play of other children and be written from the point of view of the profiled child. Children should only be identified by their first name and age and only positive interactions recorded in other children's files. More negative interactions that need to be recorded could state just 'another child' or 'a younger child'.

Parents may choose to use information on playmates to initiate further opportunities for friendships outside the setting if they wish, but this must not be influenced in more than a general way by the setting staff. However tempting it is to respond naturally when a parent is being just friendly and interested or concerned for other families, practitioners must remain professional at all times and never allow themselves to be drawn into conversation about any other children or give out or accept information that is not relevant or not only about a parent's own child.

During private consultations, practitioners must remain in control of the conversations and be aware of where some types of questions or comments might lead. Some parents may try to find out information about other families, or ask or even demand to know about the needs of another child who displays unacceptable behaviour or requires special provision, especially if they are afraid that their child may be hurt or upset or not receive their full share of adult attention. However difficult it can be to be placed in this situation, it is vital to offer these parents reassurance that all children's individual needs are being considered and met and to agree to discuss only facts that are relevant to their own children.

If parents become too demanding, upset, or even aggressive, a practitioner should leave the situation and enlist the support of the setting's manager or another staff member, waiting until emotions are under control and constructive discussion can again be attempted. Parents must be reminded that confidentiality is vital. They may sometimes need explanations as to why they might wish for this policy to be applied to their own child to enable them to understand and respect others' need for privacy.

To avoid accidental or unintended breaches of confidentiality, it is necessary to ensure that consultations cannot be overheard by other parents who are waiting and that profiles are kept private. Instead of leaving them all out on display in an unsupervised waiting area, they could be shown to parents in advance on another day, or given out by another member of staff to parents as they arrive, or kept by the key person until each consultation begins.

A few parents or carers may be unable or unwilling to attend consultations or they may appoint another person to attend on their behalf. If the manager of a setting is confident that every possibility has been considered, including a home visit for a parent who has a significant disability or is unable to leave another person that they care for, they may decide to communicate by telephone or email with that family instead.

It is important to remember that parents do not have to attend consultations or meetings about their children at early years settings if they do not wish to do so, unless their development, behaviour or safety is a cause for concern. However, the majority of parents and carers enjoy attending consultations and discussing their children's development with the other people who care for them and know them best.

By helping parents and carers to recognise and take pride in their children's progress and achievements, early years practitioners make a very valuable contribution to the lives of young children and their families, enabling them to enjoy and make the most of this vitally important time.

The responsibilities of a key person

Each child attending an early years setting will be assigned a key person who takes particular responsibility for ensuring that all of the child's and family's needs are met and for observing, assessing and recording the child's development.

Each key person also has many responsibilities towards providing a learning community for all of the children and their families, in partnership with the other members of the staff team. They will contribute to planning, during meetings and during and after sessions, before each new half-term and throughout working hours. They will carry out planned adult-led activities, adapting them flexibly to respond to children's interests and ways of developing their ideas. They will bring in resources and ensure that all activities are accessible and successful for all children. They will evaluate each session and each weekly curriculum and make further plans which build upon the experiences of various children, who may need repetition, adaptations or new challenges.

Providing equipment and resources for play and learning

Early years practitioners must respond to child-initiated play and maximise its learning opportunities by providing resources, such as toys, books, pictures, construction kits, role-play materials, puppets, dressing-up outfits, and natural, recycled and craft materials, and by joining in with games and projects. They should also provide support with activities such as jigsaw puzzles, computer programmes, models, songs and social interactions.

If practitioners are very experienced, they may already own extensive supplies of toys and equipment which they are prepared to use in the setting when appropriate. If they have children or grandchildren of their own, or younger brothers and sisters, they may have outgrown toys, games, puzzles and equipment that are still in good condition and looking for a new home, which could be lent or donated to the setting when needed. These have the advantage of being familiar to the practitioner and having already proved that they are suitable for and popular with children of this age.

Of course, each key person should also have input into choosing and ordering new resources for the setting, in discussion with the staff team, but no setting can afford to buy everything new all the time and expensive, quality materials and equipment will always be supplemented by found, recycled and borrowed items. Throughout their careers, early years practitioners must become collectors and savers of potentially useful things and develop the ability to find, gather and adapt resources for creative themes and projects and imaginative games, usually without spending much money!

During every session, staff must be aware of the needs of all children, but particularly those of their own key children, and do their best to meet them or, if appropriate, to ensure that other members of staff are doing so. Each key person will spend an enormous amount of time between sessions preparing activities, writing up observations and next steps, keeping key children's profiles up to date and advising other staff, especially any new to keyworking.

Communicating with parents and carers

While it is, of course, important to provide environments that promote the emotional security of all young children, it can be hardest to determine when this is being achieved with babies. It is therefore of crucial importance that each key person who works with babies is able to monitor the provision they are offering and be sure that they are achieving an emotionally reassuring and stimulating atmosphere and healthy, nurturing relationships with all of the children in their care. The setting manager or another senior member of staff may be responsible for monitoring this and offering help and advice as necessary.

Many early years settings offer home visits to families before children join the group. These should involve two staff members, including the key person, and be relaxed and informal. Some parents can be overwhelmed by too much

The responsibilities of a key person

Figure 7.1 Babies need a comforting and reassuring environment that meets their physical and emotional needs.

information at this stage and want to clarify just a few key points, while others will have many questions. Home visits should always be voluntary; some parents may not wish to be seen at home and this must be respected. No judgements should be made about children's family backgrounds, but seeing children at home can make it much easier to build up a fuller picture of their families and home environments and to understand the experiences that they have had and what is important to them.

If a child is experiencing separation anxiety and has to be left at a setting in a distressed state, the parent should be encouraged to telephone a short while later and talk to the key person, who should be able to offer reassurance that the child is now playing happily and explain how the child was comforted. If this is not possible, a voicemail message from the key person, or a text, an email or a note placed in the child's bag, to be passed on by the carer who collects the child from the setting, is usually much appreciated and gives the parent more confidence when next leaving the child.

Sometimes a key person will have concerns that a child is not meeting milestones, struggling in a particular area or exhibiting very challenging behaviour, or that a family is finding it hard to cope. After discussion with colleagues within the setting, the practitioner may feel that the family would benefit from contact with another professional, such as a speech therapist or a health visitor. This will need to be tactfully suggested and explained to

The responsibilities of a key person

parents and, if they agree and give permission, the appropriate professional may be contacted and asked to meet and assess the child or family.

Some advisors prefer to meet a child with a key person in an early years setting and parents may choose whether they also wish to be present during such an assessment. Others may invite a family to attend a meeting at their own premises or offer to make a home visit. Parents or guardians may ask a child's key person to be present at such a meeting or visit, or prefer to talk about it with setting staff at a later date. After any meeting, the key person's role is to continue to support the parents and liaise between them and the other professional whenever this is needed.

Sometimes, parents can expect their children to begin formal literacy and numeracy work very early and not understand how the children learn through play. Some parents can be very competitive or tactless around other parents and children. Some are embarrassed by contact with children with challenging behaviour, disabilities or special needs, while others have no idea how to control their own child's behaviour, or are shocked upon entering a setting to find that all the other children seem to be ahead of or behind their child in development. Parents may express or cover up their feelings in a variety of ways. Some will admit that they need support and ask for help; some clearly need support but will not ask for it or accept it; and some do not need it but demand it anyway! All of these clients are equally deserving of practitioners' care and attention.

A practitioner working as a key person within an early years setting must aim to be always available and welcoming to parents and carers, and willing to talk whenever approached. Sometimes this will be just for the purposes of friendly chatting: this is valuable in making parents and children feel safe and wanted and worthy of time and attention within the community of the setting, but it is also cementing relationships and mutual respect which can be drawn upon when there is a bigger or more controversial issue to discuss.

> One mother became very concerned about her daughter's toilet training and told her key person at the pre-school that she did not believe the little girl would ever stop wetting herself. The practitioner reassured her that this phase would pass. At three and a half, her daughter's development in this area was not significantly delayed and sometimes she was just too busy playing to remember to go to the toilet in time.

The responsibilities of a key person

> But, as the mother was feeling upset, the practitioner considered the situation seriously. She suggested strategies that might help the child, such as loose trousers and favourite underwear that she would want to keep dry, gentle reminders at intervals and awarding stickers for dry days that could lead to rewards of sharing extra stories or watching DVDs with her family.
>
> As predicted, the mother looked back three months later and laughed with her daughter's key person at how the problem which had once seemed so huge and overwhelming had simply disappeared.

A key person should enjoy talking with parents and carers and these conversations should include explaining how and why they do certain things, asking what the parents do with their children outside the setting and discussing what both sets of adults might do next. They will give practical help, advice and support on a range of issues, from toilet training and tantrums to early reading skills and peer friendships, to enable parents and carers to gain greater confidence in caring for, playing with, educating and enjoying their children.

These conversations should be initiated by each key person regularly, but especially when a child has made good progress; discovered something new or enjoyed a game or activity; if there are concerns about a child's health or behaviour; or if a child seems unhappy or worried. If a key person has spent time getting to know key families well and making friends with them, he or she will be able to detect real worries and sensitively give useful advice when concerns are casually dropped into a conversation.

> A teaching assistant had a very good relationship with one of her key children and his mother and was presently satisfied with the child's progress and experiences at home and school. However, the mother voiced her concerns that, aged four, the boy showed little interest in letters and numbers and in drawing or writing his name, despite reciting many favourite stories and having excellent fine motor skills when making models and using scissors.

> The practitioner spent some individual time with the boy each day, encouraging him to make marks and drawings and to use coloured pens to follow mazes and trace over shapes. As he responded eagerly, she also made copies of his favourite activities for his mother to repeat with him at home. Together, they discovered that he preferred to use darker colours and white paper, moved his head close to the activity, lost enthusiasm if figures were too small or colours too similar, and tired easily. They reached a conclusion at the same time and his mother, who was a doctor, took him for an eye test and subsequently to be fitted with glasses. With his sight improved, the boy immediately chose to learn to read and write words and began to create detailed drawings.

Not all parents will be able to say, 'I wanted to ask your advice' or 'Could you help me?' straight out or at an appropriate moment. Many will spend days or weeks wondering whether their children are developing or behaving satisfactorily or whether they have a problem and then either blurt out suddenly that they are worried or angry or not coping well, or hint around the issue and hope that it will be put into words for them.

Parents may suddenly find the courage to speak out about their concerns at a very busy or inconvenient moment, but, if at all possible, the key person should explain to colleagues and re-arrange duties in order to respond to the crisis by making time to talk immediately, privately if necessary. If this is really not possible, it will be vital to reassure the parents that their concerns are heard and understood and to arrange to speak with them as soon as possible, preferably later on the same day.

Sometimes parents may not think that their problem is very serious, or even not recognise that they have one at all, but an experienced early years practitioner may listen to them talking or observe their child or the relationship between them and know that a discussion, some advice or help is needed in order to prevent a larger issue or a crisis. It will then be the responsibility of the key person to initiate a private chat and offer any help that would be appropriate.

Those parents who agree that they need help must receive a professional response and practical support, those who are obviously suffering but deny that there is a problem or do not ask for help need it even more, while those who admit that they have a problem but then refuse help need it most of all.

Early years practitioners must care for them all without bias or judgement and encourage them to request and accept appropriate help and support for the sake of their children and families.

If specific or specialist help is requested, or a key person considers that it is needed, it will be necessary to give information and support to parents and also to speak to the setting manager, and, if appropriate, other colleagues. Sensitive information should be imparted only on a need-to-know basis and parents should always be reassured that anything they say will be treated as confidential and only shared for the good of the child and family.

If a child develops a life-threatening allergy or serious medical condition, all staff must be aware of it and enough of them trained in how to respond immediately. If two families are locked in a disagreement between themselves, senior practitioners may need to make provision for them to be separate and monitor the situation, but need not discuss the issue with more junior staff. If there are sensitive issues or personal circumstances within a family's private life, they may prefer for only their key person and the manager of the setting to know the details. Supply, bank and agency staff will only be told of matters directly affecting children on the days they are present and are required to maintain the confidentiality of all families when they are away from the setting.

Caring for babies within a setting

Babies need to make strong attachments to their parents and other primary caregivers in order to feel safe and comfortable and able to explore the environment, returning to a familiar adult when worried or distressed. Very young children are vulnerable, but develop resilience and confidence when they feel sure that their physical and psychological needs will be met and that their safety and well-being will be protected by the adults close to them.

If babies attend a childcare setting, they will need to make secure emotional attachments to key members of staff. Each key person must engage in frequent and regular respectful discussions with the babies' parents or other caregivers, in order to share information and thoughts on progress, likes and dislikes, and developing personalities.

Parents should be encouraged to describe their babies' routines at home and to bring in comforters and possessions of their own or photographs of themselves to leave with the babies. Mothers should be welcomed if they wish

The responsibilities of a key person

Figure 7.2 Babies must make strong attachments to their primary caregivers, so that they may feel safe and comfortable enough to thrive and develop.

to come into the setting to breastfeed their babies during the day. A key person must demonstrate empathy for and understanding of a baby's needs and feelings and respond sensitively to the baby, showing warmth and loving kindness. If a baby has special or additional needs, or an allergy or medical condition, this must be carefully monitored and accepted as a part of this unique child. The many care routines throughout the day, such as feeds, sleeps and nappy changes, should always be special times with the key person. They should not be rushed or looked upon as chores, but rather as opportunities to get to know each other better and to strengthen positive emotional attachments.

A key person should use his or her knowledge of each individual baby to plan interesting sensory and play experiences and offer appropriate encouragement or comfort when needed. If a baby attends a childcare setting for a number of hours in a day or days in a week and needs to be cared for by more than one adult, the senior key person should take responsibility for sharing and co-ordinating information and ensuring a consistent experience for the child and family. Secure and positive early relationships ensure that a baby's emotional development and life chances are enhanced.

Health and medication

Any practitioners working with key children who have recognised special or additional needs will be expected to undergo training to enable them to care for and support those children in a fully inclusive manner within the activities of the setting. This may involve the giving of medication or monitoring of a chronic condition, feeding by spoon or a tube, assisting with toileting or changing nappies, adapting play resources or activities, or supporting the child in beginning to participate in group play or discussions.

If a child needs to take regular medication, it must be administered at the times agreed, written down and signed by the parent or main caregiver and the key person giving the medication must ensure that each dose is given in the presence of at least one other adult and recorded at the time of giving. Both key person and witness need to sign the record that will be shown to and countersigned by the parent or carer when they collect the child.

If the child has medication to be taken when needed, such as an inhaler for exercise-induced asthma, paracetamol for a high temperature to avoid a febrile convulsion, or a cream for inflamed eczema, the key person should decide if and when it should be given, in conjunction with the child if they are old enough and well enough to understand. The same procedure must then be followed as for regular medication.

No medication should be given to a child unless it has been prescribed, recently or as an ongoing repeat prescription, for that child (not for a sibling), by a doctor. Regular or occasional medication may be given indefinitely to control a chronic condition or for a short time following a child's recovery from an infection, such as the end of a course of antibiotics, as long as it is in the original box or bottle with the pharmacy label attached. If parents wish their children to take medicines that they have purchased for minor illnesses, they must administer these themselves. Children should not be in a setting if they have an infectious disease or if they are feeling too unwell to play happily.

If a practitioner considers one of their key children to be too unwell to stay to the end of the session, or suspects that a child is displaying symptoms of an infectious disease, they need to take responsibility for contacting the parent or carer and arranging for someone to come and take the child home. Some parents may resist this, if they are busy at work or have other commitments and other children to care for, but it is important to be firm and state clearly why staff consider that the child should not stay in the setting, and ask them to find somebody who can come to collect the child.

If the person chosen to collect the child will not be a regular carer who is known to the staff of the setting, the parent will need to give their name, together with a description and details of their relationship to the child. The parent will need to tell the carer the password that they will have written on the child's registration form in preparation for such a situation, so that the carer may introduce themselves to the key person and be permitted to take the child out of the setting.

Special needs, disabilities and sensory impairments

A key person working with a child who has a sensory impairment or a physical or mental disability will need to work closely with parents and other regular carers to ease transitions and ensure consistency for the child. It will also be necessary to work with any specialist advisors who will visit the setting to observe the child and key person, monitor progress and offer ideas and support to make the setting and its activities as inclusive as possible.

Specialist teachers and advisors for the visually impaired may suggest ways of making the environment clearer for the partially sighted child, such as painting white lines onto the steps leading out into the garden, setting red chairs around the blue tables, or marking the book corner by spreading a black and white patterned rug on the floor. They will remind all staff of the need to keep the playroom floor clear enough for children with limited vision to walk safely, by asking the other children to think about where they set out toys, to leave clear pathways through the rooms and to tidy up when they finish playing, before they move away from the toys.

A specialist will demonstrate how to approach a visually impaired child slowly, how to move in gently to be close enough for the child to be aware of and focused on the face, and how to speak clearly in introduction, using names and describing an activity. For example: 'Hello Felix. It's Debbie. Are you building with the yellow bricks?'.

Teachers and advisors for the hearing impaired may suggest both play activities that do not rely on sound, and those that encourage a child to use as much hearing as is available. They will show staff how to approach children with partial hearing from the front and keep their faces and mouths uncovered when speaking. They will also offer reminders that these children will not hear

The responsibilities of a key person

who or what is behind them and will need particular supervision outside if children are running, riding on wheeled vehicles or throwing balls.

If children wear hearing aids or glasses, parents and carers will be the experts on the everyday use of these and advisors will ensure that they are working properly and being used appropriately to afford maximum benefit. The safe care and usage of these fragile and expensive items will be the responsibility of each child's key person while they wear them within the setting. If children use any form of sign language or try to mime what they want to say, the key person and other colleagues must also learn enough signs to understand and communicate fully with them, or know them well enough to interpret their mimes and encourage attempts to speak.

Advisors will work with each key person, as well as parents, to arrange for equipment needed by children with disabilities, such as wheelchairs or walking frames, tray puzzles with large handles, noisy toys, computers or extra large nappies. A key person may need to write reports or assessments to obtain equipment on loan or money to buy the resources.

Gathering information

Practitioners need to be aware of the local doctors' surgeries, clinics and health visitors, as well as social services and support groups used by the families attending the setting, and how to contact them. They must also be able and willing to find out about therapists and specialists when required. They will work with advisors and assessors, as well as the Office for Standards in Education (Ofsted) inspectors, and a key person will contribute to meetings, discussions, reports and information gathering whenever a child needs extra support or has particular or complex special needs.

It is also important to form a good relationship with the members of the area's early years team, who will be attached to a local children's centre or centre of excellence and may be asked to hold sessions, groups and classes for parents of babies and toddlers, as well as older children, in various settings.

Each key person uses unique, in-depth knowledge and understanding of key children to set up adult-led activities based on the skills and interests they have observed, then encourages children to participate and go on to initiate further play and learning for themselves. They continuously write observations on what their key children do and say and then link all of these observations to the Early Years Foundation Stage (EYFS). They also set up activities that offer the

The responsibilities of a key person

Figure 7.3 A key person provides opportunities for children to achieve their next steps and observes their progress and discoveries.

children opportunities to achieve the next steps planned for them and observe their progress and achievements while they participate.

Much of a key person's time is taken up with writing reviews and overviews of development, assessments of ages and stages reached, summaries and progress trackers. Different pieces of information are then shared with families, with other settings attended by the children, with the schools the children will go on to, with the local councils, with Early Years or Under-Fives Advisors and with Ofsted. Provided that parents have given their permission, a key person will take photographs of their key children and others engaged in activities and achieving new skills. These must be taken with a digital camera and printed out on a computer that both belong to the setting and then deleted. No practitioner may take personal photographs of the children or take a camera or computer containing such images out of the setting.

Photographs can be useful to reassure the parent of a new or less confident child who cries when left. If staff are able to show a photograph of the child laughing and playing with friends, the parent knows that they have been happy and were not distressed for the whole session. Children love to have

The responsibilities of a key person

displays of themselves in photographs on the walls, either taking part in a particular activity, out on a trip or welcoming an interesting visitor. Later, the pictures can be made into scrap books and kept in the book area for children to talk about together.

It is important to be aware that, if an early years establishment operates as a packaway setting in shared premises, displays including photographs will need to be removed when the rooms are being used by other groups. Large screens that fold out or move on wheels can be a very useful addition to these settings' furniture, as they allow displays of children's photographs, work, pictures and posters to be kept safely in a cupboard for use at future sessions.

The profiles or learning journeys that will form a comprehensive record of each child's progress and achievements, friendships, personality and development are made up of: multiple observations with links to the EYFS; regular next steps with their reviews; overviews of development; assessments, summaries and progress trackers; details of information shared with other settings and authorities; and descriptions and photographs of projects, outings and special events.

A key person must ensure that these files are kept up to date and relevant for all key children and invite parents and carers and the children themselves to add comments and observations of their own, as well as signatures. When a child leaves the setting, to move on to school or another setting, the key person will give the profile to the family to keep. Some settings like to hold ceremonies, concerts or parties, at the end of the school term in July or at the end of the academic year in August, at which each key person says goodbye and hands over profiles to key children and their families.

Childminders will be the key person for all of the children that they care for, unless they work with a partner or within a group, and may choose to provide a special last day for each individual child whenever they leave the setting and to give the profile to the child or parent at that time.

Most children and families treasure their learning journey profiles and look at them often, returning to them again and again as the children grow older, as they encourage the sharing of happy memories. Keeping this in mind ensures that practitioners will always make the effort to create attractive profiles, filled with useful and satisfying information, and will be proud to hand them out at the end of each child's time in the setting.

The roles and duties of different staff within a setting

A mixture of staff within a team makes the environment stimulating for adults and children and ensures that a wide range of complementary abilities and interests are available. It is important that all staff members can share their areas of expertise and develop their skills as individuals, while working together to ensure that the setting runs smoothly and that their clients' needs are met. Of course, there must be a hierarchy and each practitioner must understand their own areas and levels of responsibility, while respecting those of others, but it is vital that all staff members know that they are making a vital contribution to the team, whatever their job title and position within the setting.

The manager

Taking overall responsibility for the setting, its staff and clients, the manager must both run the provision on a day-to-day basis and liaise with all relevant organisations as necessary throughout the year. In order to provide high quality childcare and education, he or she must oversee all aspects of the operation and timetabling of the setting, ensuring that the best possible standards and environment are consistently maintained and that the service offered is appropriate and flexible enough to meet the needs of the families from the local communities who will use it.

The setting manager will be a member of the management team and contribute to the strategic planning, monitoring, evaluation and development of the setting. He or she will deal with queries and requests from parents and accept new children into the setting at the beginning of each new term and at other times upon request, if spaces are available, following the Admissions policy agreed by the management team.

The most important aspects of the manager's job are to create a welcoming environment for families, to see that the Early Years Foundation Stage is adequately delivered within the setting and to ensure that all principles and statutory requirements are adhered to. The manager must hold at least a level 3 qualification, but settings are increasingly looking to employ graduate leaders with relevant degrees or to provide support to their staff while they study for such degrees. It is essential that a practitioner gains several years post-qualifying experience in early years settings before taking a manager's position.

Another important part of the job is to facilitate effective communication between the staff of the setting and other professionals and organisations, in order to meet the needs of each child and family, including those with special needs and disabilities. These may include Ofsted, Social Services, the NHS Trust and others. Some children will attend more than one setting and it will be necessary to share information regularly with their other providers. Regular Ofsted inspections will be carried out and the manager of the setting will need to provide all the information requested and to receive feedback from the inspectors during their visits, before communicating it back to the staff team.

A register and up-to-date records must be kept for all children, as well as recording learning journeys and offering regular consultations with parents and carers. This feedback is needed to ensure that parents and carers are fully informed about their children's progress and development. The manager will be responsible for checking these forms of feedback, as well as for checking the maintenance of equipment and resources, such as furniture, toys, craft materials and computers, and is also accountable for the provision's day-to-day finances and its less frequent purchases and expenses.

The manager must take responsibility for identifying training needs and organising training opportunities and continuous professional development for staff at all levels and for monitoring and mentoring new staff members, students and apprentices when appropriate. He or she will take on the management, supervision and appraisal of the deputy managers, supervisors, room leaders, senior and junior practitioners and any unqualified staff, as well as supply, agency or bank staff and volunteers. If parents and carers sometimes stay to work in the setting, using a voluntary rota system, they must also be supervised, to ensure that they understand all the rules regarding the children's care and safety.

It is essential to create and adhere to policies regarding health and safety, equal opportunities, data protection and confidentiality. A manager must take the lead in planning and implementing these policies and set an example for all staff to follow, particularly in respecting the need to keep sensitive information confidential and working in partnership with families, communicating effectively and making strong and friendly but professional relationships at all levels.

It will often be appropriate to share tasks with other staff, or delegate some of them to a deputy or assistant manager, a supervisor, a room leader, a specialist co-ordinator or a child's key person. Practitioners may take on specific roles within the setting, but they will always be under the overall supervision and responsibility of the manager. Although the manager will usually be based in the setting, either working directly with the children, meeting with staff or parents or completing paperwork and telephone calls in the office, there will be some occasions on which it will be necessary to attend meetings or training courses in other places. Some managers may divide their time between two or more settings.

The deputy or assistant manager

A deputy or assistant manager will share the supervision and responsibility for the safety and smooth running of the setting with the manager. He or she will be in charge in the manager's absence and may make independent decisions on issues that cannot wait for the manager's return. They will work together on policies and procedures and make decisions on what is best for other staff, children and families.

Also qualified to at least level 3, the deputy or assistant manager will take responsibility for a share of the general business paperwork, answering some telephone enquiries, greeting visitors and showing prospective clients around the setting, and will work with Ofsted and other professionals during inspections, visits and meetings.

Early years practitioners

In some settings, especially larger ones and those which employ a number of part-time staff, there may also be a practitioner whose official title is Third in

The roles and duties of different staff within a setting

Charge. He or she will assume responsibility if both the manager and the deputy or assistant manager are absent at the same time.

Supervisors may take responsibility for different days, sessions, age groups, areas or activities. Room leaders will lead a team of staff in caring for the children within their own rooms. These children may either be all of a similar age or a mixed age group.

All settings will employ a range of staff in positions suited to their qualifications and levels of experience. These may include level 3 senior and junior practitioners, level 2 assistants and apprentices who are working towards qualifications. They may also rely, at times, upon volunteers or parent helpers, to ensure that all tasks are carried out efficiently and safely and that there are always enough adults to spend quality time with the children. To provide cover for regular staff during holidays, training courses, sickness and emergencies, settings will employ supply, bank or agency staff. These staff members will be qualified and experienced practitioners who prefer to travel to different settings to work or who do not wish to work full time.

Specialist staff

Each setting will employ one or more staff members who are the designated co-ordinators for special and additional educational needs and disabilities and for equal opportunities. These are more commonly known as the Special Educational Needs Co-ordinators (SENCOs) and the Equality Named Co-ordinators (ENCOs). These practitioners will regularly attend training days and meetings to ensure that they are always aware of the latest research, regulations and expectations in their particular fields.

If children's special or additional needs are identified after they join the setting, the SENCOs will help each parent and carer to accept and understand their diagnosis and to obtain appropriate support. They will also liaise with other professionals as necessary and work with each child's key person to plan any necessary adaptations or extra support and to ensure the best care and progress for the child and family. Through careful observations and regular assessment of these observations, a key person and a SENCO, working in partnership, can see clearly whether any children are under-achieving or under-confident or not falling within the developmental range usually expected for their age groups. They can then offer appropriate support or

The roles and duties of different staff within a setting

Figure 8.1 Settings must use books and other resources that present positive images of all cultures, disabilities and special needs.

opportunities to the children and families or consider involving other professionals to contribute to the children's development.

Families with disabilities and those from different cultures will be supported, so that they may access all of the facilities and activities provided and learn to understand and use the language of the setting, alongside their own home languages. The ENCOs will ensure that their settings use books, toys, posters, equipment and resources that reflect the diversity of the children and families who attend and the community in which they live. They may arrange for extra help or support with translation or other issues and encourage families to share their cultures with each other.

Parents and other relatives might be prepared to come into the setting to demonstrate traditional cookery, costumes, stories or songs and rhymes, or to lend resources that practitioners may share with the group. ENCOs will take responsibility for initiating this and will take care of any precious items and see that they are treated with respect and returned safely to families. They will ensure that no child or family is being discriminated against and that no child is suffering any form of abuse or neglect, through observing families carefully and offering appropriately stimulating play opportunities that encourage children to express views and opinions and participate in their own learning, within an inclusive environment that celebrates diversity amongst its staff and clients.

The key person

An appropriate practitioner with a qualification at level 3 or above will be the key person for a suitable number of children in the setting. It is also good practice to assign a buddy worker for each child, who will take over if the key person is absent. This is especially important in settings that cater for children attending on a sessional basis and employ a number of part-time staff. If a staff member or child sometimes has to change their hours at short notice, they may not always attend the setting at the same times. A practitioner may be the key person for a number of children and the buddy worker for several others.

A key person records regular observations of the children and uses them to inform the next steps that each child should aim to achieve. He or she makes assessments of the children and shares the information with the local authority and with any other settings that the children attend. The observations, assessments and next steps, along with photographs, examples of the child's artwork, drawing and writing, and comments made by the child, are presented as a learning journey or profile, in a paper or online file, and shared with each child's parents and primary carers. A key person may also oversee the observations, key children's profiles and next steps prepared by assistants who are still training, and act as a mentor to them. He or she may support students and apprentices in the workplace, help them with their college work when appropriate and offer both verbal and written reports to their tutors when they visit the setting.

Through using various different observation methods, practitioners will learn which types are most suitable for the different areas to be observed. Narrative observations provide snapshots of important moments and achievements. Target Child observations can give a detailed account of a particular time or activity. Time Sampling allows a key person to check a child's development level over a whole session. Through this type of observation, it is possible to identify that a key child who was previously quiet and appeared to be feeling shy now speaks to lots of different children during a session and has learned to confidently join in with other children's play. Based on this evidence, a key person will encourage initiating games and inviting others to join in, to further develop a child's self-confidence and social skills.

The roles and duties of different staff within a setting

Figure 8.2 Practitioners must use their knowledge and experience to assess their key children correctly and plan for them to acquire and practise new skills.

Practitioners must use their knowledge of child development, gained through training and experience, to ensure that they look for vital clues and sound evidence when observing children and that they do not miss or misunderstand important achievements, or assume that a child is at a particular level in all areas of development at the same time, without watching carefully to find out where there are any gaps. They will then be able to assess each child correctly, drawing on both their observational evidence and their years of experience in working with foundation stage children. This will enable them to identify appropriate next steps for each individual child and to plan activities and resources so that the child can acquire and practise the new skills, abilities and attitudes identified.

Using professional understanding to inform practice

Familiarity with development theory informs practice. Effective practitioners understand why the policy of each child being given a key person is so important within an early years setting. They also understand how to support

The roles and duties of different staff within a setting

Figure 8.3 Sharing observations, assessments, concerns and progress at staff meetings helps practitioners to work as a team.

and encourage children's learning within an enabling environment. Sharing observations and assessments of children's development with colleagues and discussing individual progress at staff meetings helps practitioners to work as a team. It also allows them to check their effectiveness as team members and, where applicable, as mentors and role models for less experienced staff.

Explaining practice and setting a good example for others to follow ensures that senior staff remain constantly aware of their crucial role in understanding and promoting children's development. Less experienced staff and those in more junior roles should seek to learn from good examples that they are set, to question what they do not understand or agree with and to share ideas of their own. Those who follow strong leaders will quickly gain in confidence and experience and become aware of the importance of their own roles.

Continuous professional development

All early years practitioners will be involved in continuous professional development, to explore new areas of interest, take new training courses and qualifications and keep essential skills, such as first aid and child protection, up to date. They should always seek to acquire new skills that will enable them to offer more services to the parents and children of their settings. This may mean offering new activities and experiences, such as craft projects, science experiments, outdoor games or role-play scenarios, or providing important facilities, such as parenting classes, nutrition workshops, translation services or play sessions for carers and toddlers. Training is also available for practitioners who would like to feel more confident when offering advice to families with emotional needs, handling complaints or managing difficult situations.

In-house training can take place at settings, but it can be very hard for enough staff to be available at the same time outside their working hours, especially for this type of extra work, which is unpaid, if they all have families and other commitments. For this reason, practitioners may often attend courses alone or in pairs and bring their new knowledge back to the setting to cascade it to the rest of the staff team during the hours already scheduled for meetings and preparation.

Practitioners are often prepared to lead parent support groups, but it is hard to make them fit with working sessions, while maintaining adult : child ratios and pay levels. It is sometimes necessary to arrange for these to meet during evenings or weekends and to ask parents to pay small fees and to help each other with childcare.

Young and inexperienced staff may begin working in settings as apprentices or unqualified assistants and take training courses to achieve qualifications at level 2 or 3 or above. Others may change career a little later in life, working first as a volunteer or a parent helper in a setting and going on to take a number of qualifications, over a period of years, enabling them to work in settings in various positions and eventually to lead or manage, as graduates. Their roles and duties will depend upon their position and status within the hierarchy at any particular time and the levels of qualification and experience that they have achieved so far.

Many settings allow voluntary work placements, but have to be careful to ensure that they do not impact upon the quality of the children's experiences. Students on work experience placements can be a great asset to a setting, bringing in new ideas and enthusiasm, and it can be extremely useful to have extra adults available at certain times, allowing settings to consider activities or outings that they could not otherwise carry out safely. However, students must always be mentored, supervised and supported by regular staff members,

The roles and duties of different staff within a setting

Figure 8.4 Young staff and students can be a great asset to a setting and their duties and responsibilities may be gradually increased with support and supervision from more senior practitioners.

knowing that they should ask whenever they need help or advice and that it will always be freely and happily given. Their duties and responsibilities may be gradually increased as appropriate, as their confidence and abilities grow. Students must learn and practise, but children and their families have a right to expect excellent experiences at all times.

It is important to ensure that parents and carers always receive a professional and caring service, especially at the beginning and end of sessions, and can speak with their own key person or a senior practitioner, rather than with a student, when they wish. However, they also have a right to know who is interacting with their children during the day, so details of each student's name and the course they are following should be made available and opportunities provided for parents and carers to meet students when they wish. Children may talk about their new practitioners at home and want to introduce them to their parents themselves.

Sometimes, a parent who already holds an early years qualification may join the staff team, on a supply, temporary or permanent basis. Others may choose to begin training in the field. A staff member may have been a pre-school parent last year but now is studying for an NVQ qualification, while working in the setting. Some parents may take courses in food hygiene or catering, healthcare or special needs work, having decided that they would prefer a change of career or one that fits more easily with caring for their children while they are young. Others, who recognise the needs of other families, may become registered childminders in order to offer care to other children alongside their own.

It is vitally important that children in early years settings experience caring and stimulating interactions and that they are only exposed to adults who are good role models and committed to encouraging learning and development in a happy and sociable environment.

Sensitive management of staff, colleagues and clients

The manager, deputy manager and all other senior staff within an early years setting must be able and willing to give time and effort to ensuring its smooth running, through confident and sympathetic interactions with all staff and clients. It is also vital that healthy relationships are developed and maintained between colleagues.

Relationships between adults and children within a setting are very visible and easily checked and monitored by the manager, the staff team and parents. However, the relationships that exist between members of staff are much harder to check and monitor, but also absolutely crucial to the quality and smooth running of any setting. Unhappiness, unrest, rivalry, jealousy, underconfidence, inexperience, laziness, intolerance, lack of understanding or an unwillingness to embrace change or consider new ideas must never be allowed to lurk beneath the day-to-day interactions of a staff team, hindering the improvement and development of the setting and its users.

Providing an excellent service

It is important to remember at all times that a service is being provided for clients. The needs and well-being of the children matter most and must always come first. But, for the children to be happy and successful within their early years setting, their parents or primary carers and wider families must feel that they are welcomed and supported and that their needs are being met and their wishes understood and respected, so considering and ensuring their well-being is almost as important. Although it is very important that staff are valued and fulfilled, they should remember that they are at work and that they

108

Sensitive management of staff, colleagues and clients

Figure 9.1 Practitioners must support each other and function as a team when working directly with children and their families.

should find their rewards in carrying out that work to the best of their abilities and take pride in ensuring the progress and happiness of their clients.

All practitioners must work as a team and be seen to support each other when working with the children and their families. Any issues that arise must be discussed outside session times or away from areas used by children or their parents and carers. Clients must never see or sense upsets, resentments or work not shared fairly, or feel that any practitioner is not fully committed to their tasks.

Timekeeping

The manager, deputy manager or supervisor of a setting must always arrive earlier than other staff, to open the building and to be ready to receive them and greet them warmly each day. It is best to give staff a starting time slightly earlier than absolutely needed and pay them from that time, so that everybody can arrive calmly and prepare for the session without stress.

It is acceptable to check the time as each staff member arrives and to expect a reasonable excuse if anybody is more than five minutes late. If any staff members frequently arrive late, it will be necessary to talk with them privately to discuss what could be changed to allow them to arrive on time, or how a slightly later time could be made to fit with the needs of the setting. These discussions must happen as soon as possible, especially if there is a lot of setting up to do before a session, as it is important that all practitioners share the heavier work and preparation fairly. Those who always arrive on time and move all of the furniture and equipment into place will naturally come to resent those who arrive once most of the hardest work is done, unless a solution is found.

In some settings, it may be possible to agree that most of the preparation for the next day's session is carried out before staff leave, once the children have gone home. In a packaway setting operating from shared premises, everything will have to be removed after each session and replaced for the following one, but it may be possible to arrange a rota that requires some practitioners to set out furniture and equipment at the beginning of the day and others to pack it away at the end. This could suit those who cannot arrive early but are able to stay later, as well as those who can come into work at any time but must leave in time for another commitment.

Clients in early years settings can usually be permitted some flexibility with arrival times. In a nursery, they may bring and collect their children at the times they choose and pay either for days, half days, particular sessions or by the hour. In a pre-school, they will usually bring and collect their children at set times or during the first and last half hour of sessions. Staggered entry and leaving times feel calmer for young children and their families and allow each key person more time to greet their key children and to speak with their parents and carers individually.

If a session does end at a specific time, at which clients are expected to collect their children, practitioners should endeavour to always finish their final activity and have children ready to leave within minutes of this time. It can be very difficult for some parents and carers to wait for a lengthy period in a cloakroom area if they have other children or babies, other commitments to return to or a car parked for a limited period. If they feel that they will usually have to wait, they may begin to arrive later and later at the setting or feel rushed and worried, which will affect their interactions and relationships with their children and with staff at this vital time, therefore lowering the quality of their early years experience.

When a client knows that they will arrive late or be unable to attend on a particular day, due to another commitment or appointment, they should always inform the setting in advance. They should also be encouraged to communicate with the setting manager or office by telephone or email if they have to change their plans at short notice, to allow practitioners to make adjustments where necessary. This is simply good manners and clients should be encouraged to understand that practitioners who are preparing themselves physically and emotionally to care for their children deserve to be treated with that level of respect.

However, if clients occasionally have a problem at home or on the way to the setting, or simply a difficult morning, and arrive later than expected, they must feel that they are still welcome to come into the setting with their children and know how to use a bell, intercom or telephone if necessary to gain access. Practitioners should try to improve the day for the children and families from this point by greeting them warmly, offering sympathy, understanding and reassurance and involving the children in play activities while allowing their parents or carers either to stay to talk about their problems or to rush off to work or other commitments, as they wish.

If a key person is planning a particular activity in order to observe a child's responses or offer a valuable learning experience, or a rota is operating to ensure that each child may take a turn to participate in baking, gardening, craft or snack preparation, staff need to know in good time so that they can change their timetable to accommodate a child's absence or attendance on different days. This can prevent a lot of frustration and wasted time and effort, although flexibility will always be required because there will still be days on which a child does not attend and nobody knows until the last minute, due to illness or special family circumstances.

It is also important that staff feel sure that they may leave the premises on time. They should be easily able to extricate themselves from duties at the time their shift ends, or able to complete all necessary tasks after the children leave the premises within the time that has been allotted. They should feel comfortable about walking away no more than five minutes after the working time agreed and under no pressure to stay to help with extra tasks, to tidy up for a longer period or to talk with colleagues, unless they wish to do so.

It is quite possible that some practitioners will choose to stay longer on some occasions, for various reasons, and that they may be willing to give extra time when there has been an unexpected emergency, or an urgent need arises to spend time clearing up or setting up an activity, or talking about a problem or special need affecting a client. A flexible attitude is a part of a professional working life and adults respect this. However, staff who need to catch a bus or arrange a lift to get home, or who need to collect their own children or move on to another commitment after a session, will have to leave at their set times, at least on certain days of the week, and arrange other ways of fulfilling extra duties.

A staff team may be encouraged to work together to think of ways to facilitate flexible working when particular needs arise, such as group outings or events, important meetings, appraisals or parent consultations, which require longer working days or attendance out of usual hours. They may be able to offer lifts to each other or arrange to share taxis, take turns to care for each other's children or swap days and shifts. If many practitioners live locally and encounter the same difficulties at the same times, such as school closure days or strikes for their own children while the early years setting is open, it may be possible for them to offer help to each other and solve the problems together. For example they could take turns to work in the setting and to care for all of the children at home each time the schools are closed.

Appreciation

Practitioners should always remember to thank each other. So much feeling is conveyed by the simple words and a genuine, heartfelt 'thank you' can defuse anger, prevent irritation or resentment and make a colleague feel valued and appreciated. It is important to say thank you to children and to each other frequently during sessions too, as adults must be role models and set the example for children to follow.

Managers and senior practitioners should always thank staff members and each other specifically for being flexible, working an extra shift, arriving early or staying late, taking on an extra task or duty or dealing with an unexpected problem, an unpleasant job, a difficult parent, a family needing help and support, or any other emergency. Setting leaders and supervisors should also habitually thank all staff when they leave at the end of each day or session.

When asking for help with a particular task, chore or project, it is important to phrase requests carefully, rather than giving orders or making demands. Although a staff member should understand that they are required to do what is necessary for the good of the children and the setting, they will appreciate being asked rather than told and will be more likely to perform tasks with

Sensitive management of staff, colleagues and clients

good grace or feel inspired to start and lead new topics if they know that their wishes and opinions are being considered and their contributions valued. Any person would prefer to be asked: 'Please, would you mind . . . ?' or 'Do you think you could . . . ?' or 'I was wondering how you would feel about . . . ?' or 'I was thinking that maybe we should think about . . . ?', rather than simply being told what to do.

Colleagues should work at valuing and supporting each other and exchanging experiences. Even unpleasant and difficult tasks can be satisfying when practitioners work alongside each other, offering moral support such as: 'I know what that's like! I remember when I had to do this once before. I know how hard it can be!'. Swapping tales of previous disasters managed, emergencies avoided, problems solved and catastrophes averted can allow everybody to see the funny side of working life, and can bring a team together.

Setting managers, supervisors and room leaders should err on the side of never asking a staff member to do quite as much as they do themselves. They must be clearly seen to perform all tasks, from the most menial to the most senior, and to choose the least pleasant tasks for themselves on some occasions, while delegating the more popular ones to others. Cleaning bathrooms, first aid, dealing with sick children and sweeping up sand are vital, alongside planning, teaching and paperwork, and must be shared fairly amongst all staff. There is a lot of truth in the saying: 'A good manager is not above cleaning the floor!'.

> One primary school headteacher gained the greatest respect from his staff team for two reasons. The first was because he ate his lunch early and then took responsibility for the children's first aid during every lunchtime, dealing with grazed knees and bumped heads with care and compassion while the teachers took their lunch break in the staff room. The second was because, whenever the cloakrooms flooded while the caretaker was off duty, he postponed or delegated his other duties and went to unblock the sinks and mop the floors himself.

Staff will naturally follow the example that is set by the leader of their team or establishment. They will take notice of the quality of work delivered and the commitment to ensuring a good environment for both staff and clients. They will also be aware of the number of hours and the amount of effort expended on preparation, planning, providing and problem solving. Practitioners and teachers will feel confident and inspired to do their best if their leader is talented, stimulating, dedicated, appreciative, fair and reliable. A headteacher, manager or director is a role model for adults as well as children and will reap the rewards of a hardworking and committed team if that is the example set.

> The producer of a children's theatre company arrived hours before her staff for each workshop session to unload and set out equipment; gave out clear notes and schedules to all staff in advance; allotted preparation tasks according to abilities and preferences; and spent time talking with staff members while setting up before and after every session. She also always ensured that she dealt with any first aid and sickness issues during drama workshops and rehearsals, while her staff got on with the business of teaching and performing, and took responsibility for supervision and all spillages and emergencies during lunchtimes, so that her staff had their break and time to eat. They then left in high spirits at the end of each performance, while she stayed to clean the premises and remove the equipment. Staff members were keen to stay with her for years and always gave time, energy and commitment beyond that expected or required of them.

Practitioners, children and parents appreciate and respect leaders who plan efficiently, communicate clearly, take responsibility for everything that happens, respond to emergencies calmly and always make time to care for the people and the working environment that are important to them.

Responsibilities

Practitioners need to feel that they have enough responsibilities and are needed and valued by all other members of the team. Depending upon qualifications and levels of experience and confidence, staff should be asked to assume appropriate levels of responsibility and to gradually add more challenges and extra duties. A setting leader will need to be aware of each staff members' strengths and weaknesses, abilities and preferences, and deploy them effectively, making sure chores and activities are shared out fairly and all

Sensitive management of staff, colleagues and clients

Figure 9.2 Leaders and practitioners must make time to give quality care and attention to individual children and to all of the people who are important to them.

duties are covered. If any gaps become obvious when planning rotas and curriculums, senior staff will need to cover these themselves and consider including some further training or continuous professional development for colleagues in the future.

Respect should be gained, rather than lost, when a manager or supervisor admits that other members of staff are more qualified or experienced in certain areas, such as music, singing, dance, drama, art, baking or using computers, and asks them to take on the leadership of their area of speciality. A leader does not have to be an expert in all areas of the curriculum, but must manage and co-ordinate the team members effectively, to use everybody's strengths and skills for the benefit of the children and their families. When practitioners display skills but seem under-confident or reluctant to ask for more responsibility, it is often a good idea to casually ask them to take on a particular project as a short term or single commitment and trust them to do it in their own way. Then, if it proves successful and they gain in confidence, a leader can praise them and request that they plan and lead further activities on a more regular basis.

Senior staff must avoid undermining staff or colleagues, even accidently, by watching or listening to them too closely. If it is necessary to supervise students, apprentices, volunteers or new staff, it is important to try to do so unobtrusively and not make it obvious that they are being watched and listened to all the

Sensitive management of staff, colleagues and clients

time, even if that is the case. Experienced practitioners must be trusted to make their own decisions, to deal with visitors at the front door and to handle interactions with parents, carers and families without interference from colleagues.

If staff members need to share responsibility for any issues, they should ensure that this is properly understood and discuss everything with each other as equals. There may be times when managers or supervisors feel that they must take on the responsibility for matters that other staff members were previously dealing with, because the situations have changed or turn out to demand more experience or resilience or a deeper knowledge of a particular family's needs or circumstances that may not be made available to others. Sometimes a family may request that their difficulties are dealt with by the setting leader and their wishes must be respected. In these cases, it is vital to be honest and state why the change will be made, as well as reassuring the colleagues that they are busy and that their valuable time can be better used elsewhere.

If supervisors, room leaders or other staff can have their own keys to the building and come in to set up or be left to clear up without the manager or deputy manager of a setting, they must be trusted to do so, once they have proved that they understand exactly what is to be done and how to do it. The manager must not come in anyway just to check on them, but assume that they will cope and arrive later as agreed. If he or she still feels it necessary to drop in to check the building after staff have left, the staff should not be aware of this.

When practitioners are working with small groups of children in different rooms or areas within the setting, a leader or supervisor may listen generally to ensure that there is not a riot breaking out in a group or a distressed child who cannot be comforted, but should avoid sweeping in to interfere. If there are concerns, or a new or inexperienced staff member is managing a group for the first time, a good way to check on progress and offer unobtrusive support is to arrive at each group in turn with a camera and stay for a few minutes to watch and listen, and possibly casually offer some advice, reassurance or praise, while taking some photographs.

If one or more children are exhibiting challenging behaviour, it will be necessary to find a way of moving staff around so that these children may receive one-to-one support. All practitioners should take their turns at leading groups and activities and at supporting each other and working with children with additional or behavioural needs. If a child attending a setting has special needs and has a number of funded hours of one-to-one support from a designated adult, it is good practice to name two practitioners who will share this between them, so that full-time staff may cover for each other if one is absent or part-time staff may work different shifts or on different days of the week. Time must then also be allowed for these colleagues to meet and liaise with each other and with the child's parents or other primary caregivers.

Managers and leaders should understand that they do not need to concern themselves with every small detail of daily provision. It is possible to make the best use of the mix of skills and attitudes contained within the staff team by celebrating their differences and valuing their diversity, as much as those of clients. Somebody who hovers over practitioners as they take the resources they need, counting pairs of scissors, sharpening pencils or criticising the pouring of glue into pots will quickly become exhausted and much resented by their staff. Encouraging colleagues to advise and support each other will create an atmosphere of friendly co-operation from which everybody may learn something.

It is vital to be consistent in approach and not to continuously change rules, aims or attitudes. Managers must not indulge in fads or try to follow every new idea suggested in the press. They must not suggest things without following through, so that they are unlikely to ever happen, or undermine others' planning by deciding on new activities without warning and insisting that they are provided today instead of what is outlined on the setting plan. Practitioners may have gone to trouble to source and provide supplies and make plans for activities to be presented to particular groups of children in order to observe and assess in particular areas. If this is not respected, they are unlikely to continue to make the effort.

Managers must not seek to change without reason things that were discussed and agreed at a previous staff meeting, either because they have forgotten what was said or because they want to enforce their own point of view to the detriment of others. If they make mistakes, as all humans do, they must recognise and admit that they were wrong and apologise unreservedly.

No practitioners should show favouritism to any clients at any time, whether because they are putting the needs or wishes of their key children's families above those of other clients, or because they feel intimidated by the demands or attitudes of certain parents or carers, or unable to cope constructively with a child's challenging behaviour. They must not lose sight of the setting's users as a community group, who are to be treated with equal respect, and avoid becoming obsessed with any particular person, disability, condition or special

Sensitive management of staff, colleagues and clients

educational need or responding most quickly to whoever shouts most loudly. A manager must be aware of this possibility and guard against this happening, providing reminders and advice when necessary to all members of the staff team.

Although these management points sound obvious when detailed in this way, they are not always so easy to recognise or put into practice on a day-to-day basis within a busy early years setting. There are managers who are guilty of all of them at different times and their settings suffer, as their staff teams become more and more unsettled and demotivated and eventually disintegrate completely.

Staff meetings should be as regular and frequent as possible. All staff should meet with at least some of their colleagues, outside the time they spend with the children, at least once a week and senior practitioners may meet more often. Depending on the size of the setting, it may be relevant for the whole staff team to get together or for smaller groups to meet at different times. Meetings should be kept short and discussions relevant. Chatting about issues other than work is valuable to cement relationships and friendships between colleagues, but should be monitored carefully and mostly indulged in outside working hours or while setting up or tidying rooms without the children present.

Figure 9.3 Staff meetings should be regular and frequent and allow practitioners time for relevant discussion.

Sensitive management of staff, colleagues and clients

If staff and children's parents or carers know each other outside working hours, they must be careful to maintain a professional and appropriate relationship within the setting. It is inappropriate for them to be friends through social media while linked by a parent's child attending the setting in which the carer works.

Practitioners should expect parents and carers to be responsible too. They will need to remember the things that they have been told about the rules and standards of the setting, arriving to deliver and collect their children at appropriate times each day, letting the setting know if they cannot attend and managing their children's day-to-day behaviour and well-being. Children should arrive clean, fed and ready to play and learn, bringing with them the things they will need for the day, such as spare clothes, coats, boots and packed lunches. They should be discouraged from bringing bags containing unsuitable items from home or their childminder's house.

> The children of one pre-school regularly brought large soft toys and blankets with them and some of their bags often contained dummies, sweets, drinks, money, action figures, marbles, make-up, perfumed hand gels, baby wipes or medicines! As the children had free access to their own bags whenever they fetched their coats to go outside, they often wanted to take out unsuitable items to play with.
>
> To solve this problem, the staff decided to introduce a policy of bags containing spare clothes and comforters being kept in a separate cloakroom and accessed by children only in the company of a practitioner. The children were given small book bags in which to carry only their diaries and artwork between the playrooms and home.

Parents and carers should allow their children to bring in only one comfort toy or object and must hand in any medications to staff, to be kept in a locked box and administered only according to medical instructions. If special items are brought to the early years setting, to be shown to the group during a circle or discussion time, they should be cared for by practitioners and safely returned to children when they leave. It may be necessary to explain the reasons for these rules to some parents and to remain firm for the children's sake. Once parents become used to their children attending early years settings and schools, they quickly understand the frustrations of lost or broken possessions and they usually stop allowing their children to bring in toys and other items at random, but early years providers have the task of explaining this as a new idea to many parents each year, as they introduce these families and their first children to the experience of attending a setting.

If some children appear to make their own decisions and dictate to their parents or carers more than is appropriate, practitioners can play a valuable role in re-educating the children and families. Teaching children how to speak to adults and how to achieve their wishes politely and consider others' needs is a natural part of an early years setting experience provided by dedicated practitioners: setting a correct example may bring improvements at home too. In conversation with these parents and carers, each key person should tactfully remind them that they are the adults and that they must make all major decisions for their young children, in order to keep them safe and to help them to grow up to be socially acceptable, well-adjusted people. When describing undesirable behaviour, parents often ask the question: 'Why does my child always do that?'. The best response is: 'There is only one reason that he ever did it more than once. Nobody stopped him the first time!'.

Parents must understand that they should not be afraid of stopping their children from doing or saying things that make them uncomfortable. Very few parents are actually too strict and children need and thrive on consistent guidance and boundaries. Many adults are simply inexperienced and only need guidance and reassurance to develop the confidence they need to become effective and happy parents. Families who are genuinely struggling to meet the needs of their children, either through poverty, inexperience, illness, special needs, disabilities, difficult circumstances or inappropriate attitudes, must receive the support that they need from practitioners and, where possible, be referred to other professionals and services that can help them. Conversations with these families should be conducted privately, and confidentiality maintained at all times.

Organisation

Keeping everything in its place and insisting that the adults keep their equipment and resources tidy is vital, or they will be unable to do their jobs properly. This also sets a good example to the children. Practitioners should share out the responsibility for checking essential items regularly and replacing them before they are used up. This will include vital forms, planning sheets and blank reports to be filled in, first aid supplies, disposable gloves and aprons, children's drinks and snacks, and everyday supplies such as pens and stickers.

When staff hand in completed forms, reports or contributions for children's files, it is important for leaders or managers to remember that a large amount of effort has been made, often outside paid working hours or during lunchtimes and breaks, to ensure that paperwork is ready in time for a deadline or kept up to date and regularly maintained. Many early years practitioners, especially in the private, voluntary and independent (PVI) sectors, are paid only for the hours they actually work with the children (and the time they spend directly setting up and putting away activities or attending staff meetings), but are expected, nonetheless, to also complete all the necessary associated paperwork, which takes many hours each week.

Completed planning sheets, whether prepared by practitioners independently or as a team, should be displayed prominently for all staff to refer to, while updated policies, procedures and information needed for the setting's records, for Ofsted or for individual children, must be gratefully accepted and immediately stored carefully in the correct places. This shows that appropriate and well-presented work is appreciated and respected and will be used correctly, ensuring that all staff members will continue to make the effort to give their time and professional knowledge and experience for the good of the setting and its clients.

If a manager is careless or disorganised and runs the risk of losing work, or not keeping it in a good condition until it is needed, or never asks for work on time, or fails to notice whether deadlines are adhered to or missed, practitioners will rightly feel that their efforts are wasted and find it not worthwhile to maintain high standards. If some staff members always contribute excellent work on time, while others cannot be trusted to complete their work reliably but are not even reminded of the importance of doing so, resentment will inevitably begin to build up and tensions within the staff team will cause problems.

All staff who work in a setting, even on an occasional, supply or voluntary basis, must know where everything is and be able to access whatever they need easily. There should be a cupboard that contains all of the setting's brochures, policies and procedures, enquiry and registration forms, visitor's book, forms on which to take messages and write notes when answering the telephone or the front door, registers, accident forms, medication sheets, permission slips, and contact details for other health, education and child protection professionals that can be used by staff or given to parents. This cupboard must be accessible only to practitioners and locked outside session and meeting times.

Clients need to know that their children's forms and records and any other information that they give will be safe and respected. When parents or carers return any sheets, forms or permission slips to setting staff, they must see that they go immediately to the correct place, especially if they are accompanied by payments. This may be a clipboard, a box or a folder, but it should be stored securely within the lockable cupboard.

Any messages given to a staff member must always be reliably passed on to the most appropriate person, so that clients may feel that they can safely talk to any practitioner about their child's needs or family circumstances or about particular arrangements for the child's collection. If practitioners gain a reputation for unreliability, because they forget to give a child's key person or the manager a piece of important information, clients will be reluctant to talk to them in the future. Some instances of forgetting to pass on information before handing over to another staff member could be potentially disastrous, such as when a parent has specified who will collect their child or when to administer medicine, or requested a meeting with the manager or key person at the end of the session.

All practitioners should lead by example and teach children how to use equipment and resources and then return them to their places, so that everybody will know where to find them when they are needed again. Children should learn how to explore and play in a satisfactory way, but maintain a degree of order and purpose by tidying up when they have finished and before beginning a new project. There will be times when they need to work together to tidy up and make space for a group activity, but there should be somewhere that they can leave completed pictures, games, experiments, models and work-in-progress that they would like to return to on another occasion.

It is important to view an early years setting and all the people affected by it as a community within itself. All of the adults must respect each other and work together, sharing the care and nurture of the children, to ensure that every individual is equally valued and able to thrive in a positive environment.

Rotating staff duties

The owner or manager of an early years setting, or another senior member of the staff team, will take responsibility for arranging a rota and ensuring that the correct number of adults are employed for each session, according to the numbers of children attending, to meet the legal ratios and requirements and provide a safe and constructive environment.

In some early years settings, all of the children may attend full or half time and all places may be filled. In this case, there will be a set number of staff required at all times and all staff may work the same hours, but there will often be part-time staff sharing a position and supply staff who are willing to come in to cover staff absences that occur due to illness and family commitments. A setting offering extended opening hours may require staff to work two or three different full-day shifts in rotation.

In a sessional pre-school, nursery or crêche, there may be many staff who all work different numbers of hours on different days of the week and are willing to be flexible, swapping shifts and covering for each other as necessary. This can be very successful, but can also, at times, demand a great deal of juggling logistics.

Most importantly, the person in charge of arranging staff hours and duties must know and understand each staff member and their situation very clearly. It is best to build a degree of flexibility into all contracts to ensure that staff can be asked to attend parent consultations and end-of-term events two or three times a year and to consider altering their working hours or days if they are given a term's notice of the changes. It is also reasonable to expect all staff to help in any way they can in a crisis. But, it is essential to be sure of who wants to take on more hours whenever they are available and who does not want to be asked to work extra hours very often. Some practitioners have more time to spare or need to earn more money when they can, while others have busy lives and prefer to work only regular part-time hours.

A manager should make it clear to all staff that they can ask to swap or miss a shift if they need to, but that they can always say no when asked to swap a day or work extra hours without having to give an excuse. Most practitioners will understand that, if they occasionally agree to swap a day or work an additional shift to help a colleague, they will feel able to ask someone else to do so if they ever need the same help. This should be monitored in an unbiased way, so that it is noticed if one person takes more time off than everybody else or asks to swap shifts too often. If so, it may sometimes be necessary to have a private chat about their needs to find out whether a different shift pattern, a change of days or a reduction in hours would be more appropriate to their current situation, either temporarily or permanently.

Knowing the staff team as individual people is vital, to avoid some staff always giving in and doing what suits others or being over-sympathetic and always doing more than their share of the work, while others coast along making more minimal effort and allowing others to shoulder some of their hours or responsibilities too often. If a practitioner has another immovable commitment on a particular day, such as teaching a class on a Monday afternoon or running a toddler group on a Friday, it is important to remember this and avoid asking them whether they could work at this time. If some have their own children to collect, it is unfair to ask them to consider staying later one afternoon, unless they are able to discuss it well in advance and consider making alternative arrangements for their own family.

When setting leaders identify practitioners who are totally reliable and remain willing to cover for others but never ask to swap or reduce their own hours, they could consider a private chat from time to time, during which they offer thanks and state how valuable such a contribution is and perhaps make an offer of a few hours off as a bonus for excellent service. This is an effective way of keeping self-esteem and morale high and ensuring that such reliability continues and is copied by other staff members.

Salaries in the early years profession are seldom high, with many practitioners paid low hourly rates and only for the hours they work, meaning that many earn nothing at all outside term times. However, they will be aware of the remuneration offered when applying for a job and decide whether they can accept it on that basis. The difference that an employer can make is to ensure that staff are always paid on time, without delays or confusions, with any adjustments of hours correctly calculated, and with thanks.

Tasks must be allotted carefully to be as fair as possible. The best staff should not always be given the worst jobs just because others cannot cope with them or there is nobody else available at a particular time! It is better to adjust timings or to encourage other practitioners to learn by working alongside more experienced staff members until they feel confident enough to undertake the tasks alone. If one person is always given an unpleasant or difficult job and feels that this is unfair, they may even decide to move on. Whether they choose to leave the setting for this or any other reason, there will be a problem if nobody else is able to take over. If there are occasionally a few tasks that only one or two practitioners are qualified or skilled enough to do, this must be discussed in advance and their contribution regarded as invaluable, so that they feel appreciated as the best person for the job; but others should be trained or involved as soon as possible.

It is important never to take anybody for granted, as we all thrive on thanks and need to feel valued, but some people naturally expect to be thanked more often or need more praise and encouragement to stay on task, while others are more self-motivated and expect to work independently without any fuss being made. It is vital to know the members of a staff team well and to offer the right amount of support, respect and appreciation to each one.

Variety within a staff team is good for the adults and for the children. A mixture of ages and experiences can be invaluable for coping with the different families and situations that a setting will encounter. Younger staff and students may be enthusiastic and keen to try out new ideas and have great reserves of energy and stamina, but need to continuously learn from their own experiences and the advice and examples of their senior colleagues. More mature practitioners, working at any level within the setting, may have many years of experience in different settings to draw upon and a greater confidence in dealing with families, especially those who need reassurance and support or are coping with extra problems or challenges within their lives; and they may feel stimulated by the vitality of their more junior colleagues and encouraged to continuously explore new boundaries within their day-to-day interactions with the children.

Children may receive a more balanced approach, within a calm and organised but exciting and stimulating environment, when older and younger staff from different walks of life work together co-operatively, supporting and learning from each other, for the benefit of the families in their community. Parents, grandparents, nannies and childminders, if working as voluntary helpers within a setting, may sometimes be able to offer reserves of experience that can help staff to gain an extra insight into the problems faced by a child or family or a greater understanding of their needs or responses.

Supply or bank staff or volunteers, who visit the setting for regular or occasional sessions, may provide opportunities for different activities, or teach existing staff new skills that they can go on to use with the children at other times. Within a chain of nurseries or crêches, there may be opportunities for staff to move between settings, or to work in more than one each week or month, to provide cover for each other or to create a working pattern that equates to full-time hours. Some practitioners will enjoy the chance to do this, while others may be reluctant. It is important to know who would relish the opportunity and who would prefer not to be asked to consider it. If one of the settings is struggling more than others and has acquired a reputation as a difficult place to work, a manager or administrator could seek out practitioners who thrive on new challenges and present making positive changes as an achievable goal.

Parents and other primary caregivers

Most children have one or two parents as their primary caregivers, but others may be mostly cared for by grandparents or other relatives, nannies, childminders or other guardians. Some may be in foster care or recently adopted. Some of these adults will be more experienced and confident than others and some will find it easier than others to talk about their feelings in relation to their children attending the early years setting.

It is vital that practitioners always strive to see situations from the point of view of the parents and guardians, taking into account the fact that they may not have the professionals' level of background information or their knowledge of other clients' needs and will form opinions, think, speak and react according to what they see and hear or glean from their own children at home. Remembering also that their children are very young, and may easily misunderstand or misinterpret the actions or feelings of others, will help practitioners to attach importance to offering more details and explanations to parents and carers whenever necessary.

It may be easier for staff members who are parents themselves to imagine how other parents will feel and how certain incidents and activities will appear to them. Those practitioners who are not parents may need to ask for advice at times when considering a new initiative or dealing with a tricky situation, demand or complaint. Some useful ways of avoiding potential parental worries or conflicts are to take careful note of all instructions and all permissions given or withheld for children, to stick to the policies and procedures described in the parents' brochures and to be prepared to spend time explaining an issue to any parent or carer whenever they ask a question.

Whenever a practitioner is unsure of how parents feel about a policy or of how they would prefer for an issue to be managed, the best thing to do is to ask them. An honest face-to-face conversation or telephone call between adults can usually prevent conflicts, solve disagreements through negotiation and preserve healthy relationships. A policy of talking to each other whenever somebody senses potential differences of opinion or emerging unrest is a valuable example to set to parents and children.

If a key person considers that a child is not coping well with the hours spent in the early years setting, a discussion with the primary caregiver should be requested as soon as possible. If children are struggling because they are too young or too tired, it may be possible to reduce the number of hours or sessions, at least temporarily, and build them up again gradually as their confidence and stamina grow. If older children's behaviour is deteriorating because they have been attending the same setting for a number of years, they may be bored or under-stimulated. Talking with parents should happen before disruptive behaviour becomes a habit, to discover more about children's current interests and passions outside the setting, in order to provide new engaging and absorbing activities.

Some children prefer not to have a parent stay at the setting, particularly as they grow older, and can exhibit challenging behaviour if a primary caregiver is present. These parents and carers should be reassured that this is not an abnormal reaction and encouraged to offer their support to the setting in other ways. Other children love to have their parent or carer stay with them, but demonstrate very different behaviour or stop joining in with their friends

---

A boy moved to a new village and joined a pre-school at the age of four years. He demonstrated advanced skills in all areas and settled in quickly. However, when his mother brought his younger sister for a visit and stayed to help at the setting one afternoon, his attitude changed completely. He wandered between activities, laughed at other children, dropped craft materials on the floor, argued with his sister and displayed none of his usual concentration, advanced thinking or social skills.

Observing that this behaviour was worrying his mother, his key person encouraged her to take his sister to play out in the garden while she spent some individual time with him, playing a maths game that he particularly enjoyed and talking about why he felt uncomfortable with his family being present at his school. She was then able to explain his feelings to the mother, reassure her that this behaviour was not typical of her son in the setting on other days and suggest that she should show her support by attending events and providing items instead of helping in person, at least for the present time.

Sensitive management of staff, colleagues and clients

Figure 9.4 Practitioners will offer ideas for new activities to parents, so that children may go on learning at home.

at these sessions. Practitioners need to explain the situation and tactfully request that the adult temporarily takes on some tasks in the kitchen or another area, returning later to observe their child playing and interacting with peers as usual.

It will be necessary to vary explanations and discussions to suit the levels of understanding appropriate to different clients. Some will enjoy small details of activities and events, while others will prefer a simple overview. Some will be interested in exactly how and what their children are learning from each experience, but others will be glad to entrust much of the learning and stimulation to the professionals within the early years setting. Practitioners should get to know their families in order to meet all of their needs effectively, but will aim to offer ideas to them all, so that they may help their children to go on learning at home and all adults can work in partnership to support the children's progress and well-being.

Experienced practitioners will know that, when introducing a new initiative to a group of families or planning a community event, it is worth identifying the natural leaders and working hard to convince them of its value. If they take up the idea and run with it, the job is half done! In any community, certain individuals emerge as natural leaders and those who will take risks and offer opinions first, while others enjoy all new ideas and are always willing to get involved in projects and share the work and organisation of events. Those who are more reluctant to make changes, or less confident to embrace new challenges, can be encouraged to follow the leaders and take a smaller role that will still contribute to the project's success. A true community effort can then be achieved for the benefit of all.

Handling transitions and moving on

The lives of children and their families are a series of changes and transitions. While children are very young, many parents find their need for constant care and attention tiring and overwhelming at times. They may think that life will become easier when the children are a little older. If they say this to the staff in their early years settings, the practitioners may seek to reassure them and warn them against wishing this precious time away.

When speaking honestly with their clients, the practitioners will tell them that being a parent never gets easier, but that the types of needs and demands encountered change frequently. Over the years, the task becomes less physical and more intellectual, but it is always emotional. Different families find the challenges of primary school, secondary school or beyond to be easier or harder, as they seek to cope with their children's relationships with peers and other adults during these stages. Alongside education, they will also be managing the experiences and demands of any groups, clubs or activities in which the children participate, supporting them through excitements, disappointments, struggles and frustrations and considering the financial implications of all the choices they make.

However, all changes are very gradual and most parents cope more and more easily as their confidence grows and their responses become more natural and automatic. Having the support of family members and friends is very important, as well as that of the professionals who share the care and education of the children. Early years practitioners may find that the best advice to give to parents is: 'Enjoy every stage with your children because it will soon be gone and you can never have it back'.

Entering a new early years setting

Children may join an early years setting at any age and this may be their first experience of separation from their primary caregivers. Practitioners must be sensitive and welcoming to all members of their families and any other important guardians or carers, such as nannies, childminders or foster parents, and work hard to make the new experience positive for everybody.

Parents and carers should be encouraged to stay with their children and settle them gradually into the setting during a few sessions spread over several weeks if they wish, possibly leaving them for short periods at first until they both feel confident. However, some parents need childcare because they have work or other commitments and they may need to settle their children quite quickly, after an initial visit, and access full-time care from the beginning. Practitioners must support all families to make the best choices and arrangements to suit their own needs. Each child and family will be assigned a key person within their new early years setting, who will care particularly for their needs and wishes and ensure that constructive communication takes place every day. The aim is for all adults in the child's life to form good relationships and to work together to meet the needs of the child.

Some parents may feel very anxious or upset about leaving their children for the first time and will need support and reassurance. If children show distress at being left in an unfamiliar place with new carers, parents may also become distressed and reluctant to leave the children, or they may react with impatience or annoyance and tell the children not to behave in this way, or they may affect indifference and leave quickly. These are not necessarily indicators of the relationships between different parents and children, or of how much they care, but are all coping strategies and must be recognised and accommodated as such by the setting staff.

Parents and guardians should never be allowed to feel that it is wrong to be sad when their children first learn to separate from them confidently, but they must be helped to feel proud at the same time. Practitioners should explain that children can only achieve independence and make confident progress through life by building upon the strong foundations of excellent early experiences and loving care. They must also emphasise that children's families and primary caregivers will always continue to be the most important people in their children's lives.

During their early years, children may attend more than one setting and have several caregivers. This may mean a series of transitions or managing

Handling transitions and moving on

several experiences simultaneously. In these cases, each key person will communicate with the others and they will share information, observations and assessments with each other, as well as with the child's parents and other home-carers. Some children may accept new people and places easily and happily and appear to take transitions in their stride, while others struggle more obviously with each new set of circumstances; but no child is unaffected by a change of caregiver or setting and all need support and understanding.

New experiences can be stimulating and enjoyable at any age, but are always tiring and can be very time and energy consuming. It can help the children's parents and other primary carers if the staff of their new setting explain to them that, while the children are coping with a transition, they may temporarily regress in some areas at home and will need extra security and reassurance. If they start to ask for help with dressing or tidying up, for example, this behaviour is quite normal. They may be checking that their families will always be there to meet their needs and that they will not be put under pressure to grow up too quickly or too suddenly at home, or they may simply be feeling exhausted. As long as they are comforted and reassured that they may gain independence at their own pace, this stage is likely to be temporary and a stepping stone to enhanced skills and a deeper relationship.

Within larger early years settings that offer care for a range of ages, it may be necessary for children to move to different rooms as they mature, especially when leaving the baby rooms to join the tweenies or toddlers. A key person will often move up with children and work in different areas of a setting during different years, but this is not always possible, especially when the key children are not all of exactly the same age, and sometimes it will mean a new key person at the same time. Some children and parents will find this transition easier than others and some will move on quickly while others will want to keep returning to the security of their previous situation, but, if staff work together closely and children are allowed to make the changes gradually and at their own pace, they will all manage it successfully with time.

Preparing for school

During the academic year in which they have their fourth birthdays, children will gradually be prepared for their transition to a first, infant or primary school. Their parents or guardians will be able to visit schools in order to choose those at which they would like to apply for a place. Schools will arrange a series of visits for their prospective new entrants, in small groups, some with parents or carers and some with the staff of their early years settings. There may also be opportunities for the school reception or foundation classes to visit the early years settings and also to invite the younger children to join them for some events or outings.

A tense period of waiting and hoping may follow the application process, during which parents are anxious that their children might not be offered a place at their first choice school. Some schools are over-subscribed and families may face the prospect of travelling to a school out of their catchment area or going to one where they will know nobody, while their friends attend another school which they would have preferred. The staff of early years settings do not usually look forward to the day on which families find out the decisions that have been made! Inevitably some parents may find that they have not been awarded a place at their chosen school and will be disappointed or upset. There can also be tensions and discomfort between parents who have their first choice, and feel guilty that they cannot help their friends, and those who have not been awarded a place at their preferred school, who feel angry and unfairly treated.

Although places are allocated by the local authority and neither early years nor school staff can have any influence over the process, practitioners can offer a great deal of support and reassurance by listening to families' concerns and allaying their fears that their children could not be happy in another school. They can offer practical help by encouraging parents and children who will be starting at the same schools to spend time together during the summer term, and possibly during the holidays too, so that there will be at least a few familiar faces for them to look out for in the playground and classroom in the first week of the new term.

Most importantly, practitioners can spend extended periods talking with the children about the people and experiences they might find at their new schools. The children should hear about what they will be able to play with and how they will have lunch, use the toilets, find their coats and ask for help when they need it. It is important that staff paint as positive a picture as possible about the new settings to which their children will move, so that the children feel excited and ready to cope, rather than bewildered, overwhelmed and worried. Of course, some children will be anxious or fearful, but a child who is worried must be encouraged to talk about their concerns with their key person and given time and privacy to do so.

Handling transitions and moving on

Practitioners should accept all worries and fears as very real and important to the children and aim to give clear explanations, descriptions and examples of how to handle different situations. If children are afraid of getting lost on the way to the toilets, they may be told that an adult will show them the way each day until they are sure that they know where to go. If they are worried about putting on their own clothes or shoes after PE lessons, a key person might arrange practice sessions at the setting and also suggest to all parents that their children are encouraged to practise dressing and undressing frequently at home before the school term begins. If they think that they will be scared at lunchtimes or in the playground, they can be helped to see that eating snacks at pre-school, sharing meals at nursery or playing out in the garden is almost the same experience. It may just be a little noisier at school, because there are more children, but they will quickly get used to it.

Although some parents may think that their children need to be able to read, write, add up numbers, run, sing and sit perfectly still in order to be successful at school, early years practitioners must advise them on what is really important. During the last term before school, children in early years settings will be taught how to take care of their own personal needs and how to ask politely for help whenever they need it. They will be encouraged to

Figure 10.1 Children should be given opportunities to practise putting on their outdoor clothes independently before starting school.

learn how to recognise their own name labels; pay attention to a story, singing or discussion session within a group; choose their own play activities; take care of toys, equipment and resources; and consider the needs and wishes of others around them. A good level of maturity and confidence within their physical, emotional, social and communication development will ensure a smooth and productive start to the next stage of their education and their future learning.

Once school places have been decided by the local authority, a more structured set of visits will be arranged, so that children can become more familiar with their school buildings, playgrounds, classrooms and staff, and meet their teachers and teaching assistants. Early years practitioners will accompany groups of children on some of these visits and have an important part to play in ensuring that they go smoothly and provide a positive and enjoyable experience.

Practitioners must inform parents and carers of plans well in advance, and arrange for children to be delivered to, and collected from, the school or the early years setting at appropriate times. During the summer term, the children may be invited to take a packed lunch into the school and eat there, with their own practitioners, or they may be invited to accompany a reception or foundation class on a walk around the outdoor area or to a nearby park. Parents and carers must be asked and reminded to provide lunches, coats or boots for the appropriate days, and practitioners should also have spares ready in case a child needs them.

Taking a group of children into their school classroom for free play activities also provides an opportunity for early years practitioners to talk confidentially with the teacher and other school staff about each child and family. This could be a good time to discuss any particular needs or potential challenges that will affect some children's transition into the school.

Reception and foundation class teachers are often given time to visit the early years settings that most of the children of their new class presently attend. They may read stories, sing songs and share a snack time with the children, then chat with them during free flow activities. Practitioners should prepare carefully for these visits, by explaining who the teachers are and letting the children practise saying their names, talking about when they will come to the setting and what they might do and say, and discussing the things that they might leave at school for their classes to do with other teachers. It might also be a good idea to suggest and prepare some songs that the group could sing to the teachers and to remind the children that it will be important to say hello, goodbye and thank you. Throughout the visits, practitioners will need to guide the children and stay close to those who need more support, as some will become over-excited and others will be shy or worried.

Teachers should also appreciate time to talk privately with each key person in turn and make notes, in order to identify how best to help each of the children to settle in, develop and progress once they join their new school. Setting staff should facilitate this by arranging staff cover in advance or by planning group activities and ratios which can be safely led by the adults still working while one is otherwise occupied.

The most important aspect of this transition period is the early years practitioners' relationship with their children and the information, support and reassurance that they can give to inspire self-confidence and self-awareness. Some children may be excited and eager to move on, while others may feel anxious and upset to leave their present setting. Some may not yet understand what will happen or where they will go.

If they already have older siblings at the school, or if they regularly go to collect older children with a relative, friend, childminder or nanny, they will be more knowledgeable and confident. First and only children often find transitions to new settings and situations harder, as they are breaking new ground for their families, but they may anticipate the next stage with optimism. Second and subsequent children usually move on more easily, if they join their brothers and sisters or follow an established path for their family, but they can be adversely affected by the opinions of their siblings or parents and guardians, if they are already unhappy or dissatisfied with some areas of the school.

Staff changes

When practitioners need to leave their jobs and move on from settings, it is often ideal if it can be at the end of an academic year, when some or most of their key children may also be moving on to school or another setting, as this can avoid disruption and difficulty for the majority of families. But this will not apply to those who work with the youngest children and, even in pre-schools, there will usually be some younger children and their families who will be affected by the changes ahead. Many practitioners will find the last weeks, once colleagues, parents and children have been informed of their leaving, quite a difficult and emotional time.

Handling transitions and moving on

Although parents may initially be upset, or even angry, that they will have to get used to a new key person and build a new relationship, adults should understand that people have lives outside their work and that such decisions are made for valid reasons. Young children will not find it so easy to understand and accept a trusted adult's decision to leave, but they are adaptable and, relying on the consistent support of the other members of the setting and their families, they will cope and quickly adjust to the new situation. It may help if they can be told in simple terms and given an explanation, such as: 'She's leaving to have a baby of her own' or 'He's going to move to a new house that's a long way away'.

Sometimes, however, the reasons are less simple or more personal and clients have no right to know why staff are choosing to leave. But parents and carers do have the right to be given reasonable notice of a practitioner's or manager's intention to leave the setting, unless the resignation occurs in response to a sudden emergency or crisis, and they should also be informed of any new arrangements and of who their new key person or manager will be as soon as possible. Practitioners should make themselves available to talk

Figure 10.2 All children must be given the skills and the confidence to meet new challenges and experiences with enthusiasm.

with and reassure families as appropriate and spend time supporting children through the period of change.

The most important thing for early years practitioners to consider is that, however long or short a time they spend in a setting, they are the children's safe and secure foundation during their early years, from which they will venture out into the wider world. Through loving care, encouragement and stimulation, children should be equipped with the skills and the confidence to meet each new challenge and embrace each new experience.

It is the duty of all settings to strive to provide supportive and inspiring learning communities for the children and families that they serve.

References and further reading

Books

Chalmers, D. (2015) *Drama 3–5.* 2nd edition. Oxon: Routledge.

Chalmers, D. (2014) *Speaking and Listening Activities for the Early Years.* Dunstable: Brilliant Publications.

Fleer, M., Edwards, S., Kennedy, A., Ridgway, A., Robbins, J. and Surman, L. (2006) *Early Childhood Learning Communities – Sociocultural research in practice.* Australia: Pearson Education.

Riddall-Leech, S. (2008) *How To Observe Children.* 2nd edition. Harlow: Heinemann.

Riddall-Leech, S. (2003) *Managing Children's Behaviour.* Harlow: Heinemann.

Sheridan, M. D. (1980) *From Birth to Five Years: Children's developmental progress.* 7th edition. Windsor: NFER-Nelson.

Government documents

Department for Children, Schools and Families (2008) *The Early Years Foundation Stage: Setting the standards for learning, development and care for children from birth to five.* Nottingham: DCSF Publications.

Department for Education (2012) *Statutory Framework for the Early Years Foundation Stage: Setting the standards for learning, development and care for children from birth to five.* London: Early Education.

References and further reading

Magazines

Chalmers, D. (2014) 'Caring for brothers and sisters'. *Child Care.* January 2014: pp.12–13.
Chalmers, D. (2014) 'When accidents happen'. *Practical Pre-School.* November 2013: pp.12–13.
Engel, L. (2012) 'All about . . . UW: People & communities'. *Nursery World.* 16–29 June 2014: pp.21–25.
Hart, K. (2015) 'Involve parents at every step'. *Practical Pre-School.* April 2015: pp.22–24.
Hughes, A. M. and Read, V. (2013) 'All about . . . Building positive relationships with parents'. *Nursery World.* 18 November–1 December 2013: pp.19–23.
Jefferies, T. (2014) 'People matter the most'. *Early Years Educator.* Volume 15(2): June 2013: pp.21–23.
O'Connor, A. (2015) 'Key person approach: Providing a secure base'. *Practical Pre-School.* January 2015: pp.18–19.
O'Connor, A. (2012) 'Prime time . . . UW: Personal, social and emotional development'. *Nursery World.* 23 July–5 August 2012: pp.19–23.
Stewart, N. (2012) 'Prime time . . . UW: Communication and language'. *Nursery World.* 20 August–2 September 2012: pp.15–21.

Online articles

Better Brains for Babies (2015) 'Brain anatomy and brain development timeline'. Available from: www.bbbgeorgia.org. [Accessed: 21 February 2015]
Colbert, J. (2008) 'Brain development research can influence early childhood curriculum'. *Early Childhood News.* Available from: www.earlychildhood news.com. [Accessed: 21 February 2015]
Dunst, C. J., Hamby, D., Trivette, C. M., Raab, M. and Bruder, M. B. (2000) 'Everyday family and community life and children's naturally occurring learning opportunities'. Sage Journals Online: *Journal of Early Intervention.* Volume 23(3): July 2000: pp.151–164. Available from: www. jei.sagepub.com/content/23/3/151. [Accessed: 25 February 2015]
Rogoff, B. (1994) 'Developing understanding of the idea of communities of learners'. Taylor & Francis Online: *Mind, Culture and Activity.* Volume 1(4): pp.209–229. Available from: www.tandfonline.com/doi/abs/10.1080/10749039409524673. [Accessed: 25 February 2015]

Schiller, P. (2010) 'Early brain development research, review and update'. *Child Care Exchange*. November/December 2010: pp.26–30. Available from: www.childcareexchange.com/library/5019626. [Accessed: 21 February 2015]

The Urban Child Institute (2015) 'Baby's brain begins now'. Available from: www.urbanchildinstitute.org. [Accessed: 21 February 2015]

Index

abuse 45, 47–50, 101
access 2, 6, 18, 45, 101
accidents 28, 41, 62
accounts 27, 98
achievements 83; levels 74–7; next steps 78–81
activities 2, 70; communities 5–7, 105; homes 8–9, 23, 76–7; settings 55, 62, 69, 74, 78, 84, 126–27
additional needs see special needs
advice 1; colleagues 85, 98–9, 102–06, 113, 117, 125–26; families 25, 87–90, 94, 105
agency staff see supply staff
allergies 6, 12–13, 18, 90
alliteration 58
animals 6, 41
appointments 6, 52, 81
appraisals 26, 31, 34, 98
appreciation see thanks
apprentices see students
art see crafts
assessment 52, 69–71, 73–81, 87, 96, 100, 102–03
attachments 90
attendance 21, 27

babies 85; families 94; settings 90–1
bank staff see supply staff

behaviour 111; children 69, 86–7, 116–17, 127; parents 119–20, 137; staff 109–10, 113
beliefs 7, 13
BESD 39
books 11, 56, 64, 66, 70, 84, 101
brain research see research
brochures 3, 28, 121, 126
buddy worker 51, 102

chairperson 26, 30
challenges 44, 55, 59, 62–3, 125–26, 129
charities 33
child protection 48, 105
childminders 6, 11, 20–1, 76, 96, 107, 125–26, 131
choices 23; children 40, 62, 66–9; families 6–7, 36, 132–33
classes 19–20, 94, 105
clients 35, 97–9, 108–11, 117, 121–22, 128
colleagues 53–4, 80, 86, 89–90, 108–10
comforters 90, 119
commitment 38; families 34, 110–11, 114, 119, 120; staff 112, 124
committees 23, 25–8, 30, 33–4

142

Index

communication 13–17; children 47, 58–9, 133, 135; colleagues 34, 98, 131; families 4, 85, 120
Communication and Language 58
community 1, 13, 22, 128–29; parents 23–5, 36; settings 97, 101, 122
complaints 31, 40, 49, 105, 126
computers 32, 57, 64, 84, 95, 98
confidentiality 28, 83, 90, 99, 120
construction 56–7, 64, 84
consultations 6, 30, 81–3, 98
continuous professional development 31, 48, 98, 104–05, 115
conversations *see* communication
cookery 5, 19, 101
co-operation 1, 62, 117
courses *see* classes
crafts 19, 56–7, 64, 66, 78, 84, 105
CRB checks *see* Disclosure and Barring Service (DBS)
crisis 21, 89, 123, 137
cultures 5, 7, 12, 24, 101

decisions 27, 66–9, 99, 120
development 2, 53–5, 74, 87, 95, 97–8, 100–04; choices 67; EYFS 57–62; play 64; stages 71–2
differentiation 63–4
disabilities 17–18, 38; children 37, 47, 53, 61, 87, 93–4, 101; parents 7, 18, 77, 83; staff 26
discipline 3, 26
Disclosure and Barring Service (DBS) 26, 43, 48
displays 8, 17
diversity 11, 13, 22, 24, 34–5, 69, 100–02
dolls 14, 47, 64
donations 32
dressing up 79, 84, 101

EAL 39
early learning goals 78–80

emergencies 29; families 21; settings 111
ENCOs 11, 40, 100–01
environment 49–52, 85, 97–8, 104, 107, 113–14, 122, 125
equality 26, 37–8, 40, 99
equipment 27–8, 84–5, 94, 98
evaluation 52, 84, 97
events 27, 56, 129
experiences 9, 23, 132
experiments 60–1, 64, 105
Expressive Arts and Design 61–2
EYFS 38–9, 41, 63, 73, 80, 94–6, 98

fees 27–8, 31
festivals 12–13
first aid 41, 45, 105, 120
flexibility 21, 97, 110–12, 123
food 5, 13, 41–3, 62, 67
forms 29, 120–22
foundation class *see* schools
friendships 24; children 20, 53, 81, 95; families 20–1; staff 118–19
funding 28, 32–9
fundraising 27, 31

games 56, 84–5, 62
grandparents 11, 20, 125–26
grants 32
guardians 6, 126, 131–32
guidance 3, 31

health 41, 62
health and safety *see* safety
health visitor 86, 94
hearing impairment 18, 93–4
home visits 85–7
hygiene 28, 43, 62, 107

illness 7, 28, 31, 41, 90
incidents *see* accidents
inclusion 7, 37–41; culture 12–14; families 19–22; information 11; language 13–17; observations 69,

Index

102; specific needs 17–19, 37–41, 93
independence 3, 9, 15, 47, 62, 79, 134–35
Independent Barring Board 49
individual needs 6–7, 13, 22, 26, 71, 73–4, 83
information 82, 121–22; parents 3–4, 8; staff 29, 64, 74, 94–5, 102
inspections 31, 99
insurance 27, 43
interests 10, 23, 55, 127
intolerances 6, 12–13, 18
intuition 52

key person 3, 29–30, 51–3, 62, 73, 78–81, 102–04, 131–32; attachments 90–2; communication 85–90; resources 84–5; specific needs 92–4

language barriers 3, 7, 13–17, 101
lateness 110–11
LEA 38
leadership 97–100; adults 35–6, 115, 128–29; children 58, 61; staff 40, 51
learning journeys see profiles
legal requirements 33, 37, 40, 63, 122
legislation 37
letters 3, 21, 27, 29, 33
Literacy 3, 59, 80, 87
LSCB 49–50

malleable materials 5–6, 26–7, 30, 34, 56
management 31; committee 5–6, 26–7, 30, 34; setting 97–9
mark making 56, 59
Mathematics 60, 79, 87
maturity 40, 135
medication 41, 45

meetings 99; parents 20–1, 27, 87, 92, 94, 119; staff 51, 118
messages 122
milestones 86
mime 15, 94
models 78, 84

nannies 6, 11, 20, 76, 125–26, 131
neglect 48, 50, 101
negotiation 3, 67, 126
next steps 70, 74, 78–94, 102
notices 3, 17, 29–30

observations 52, 69–71, 73–81, 94, 96, 100, 102–03
Ofsted 31, 38, 40–2, 77, 94–5, 98–9, 121
organisation 27, 120–22
outdoors 58–9, 62, 64, 105
outings 5, 7, 27, 45, 96

parents 106–07 126–27, 130; communication 85–9; consultations 81–3; managing settings 23–30, 33–6; participation 1–10; profiles 76–8; responsibilities 119–20, 131–33
permission 29, 126
Personal, Social and Emotional Development 57–8, 79, 135
photographs 29, 43, 74, 78, 90, 95–6, 102, 116
physical contact 46–50
Physical Development 58–9
PLA 27, 30
planning 49, 51, 57–62, 72, 84, 91, 97, 117, 121
policies 3, 27–8, 30–1, 37, 121, 126
practice 52, 103–04
preferences 6, 10, 12–13
premises 18, 20, 27–8, 33, 45, 48
privacy 13, 83

Index

problem solving 7–8, 59–61, 114, 133–35
procedures 27–8, 30–1, 45, 49, 121, 126
profiles 64, 73–83, 96, 102
progress 23, 62, 70–1, 73–81, 98, 100–04
puppets 57–8, 84
puzzles 56, 84–5

qualifications 25, 31, 50, 98–100, 105–06
questionnaires 3

reception class *see* schools
recycled materials 9, 57
registration 27, 84, 98
regulations 31
relationships 1, 3; children 61, 91, 130, 136; colleagues 94, 108, 113–18, 121; families 9–10, 61–2, 76, 87, 99, 131–32
reliability 4, 50, 112
religion 7, 12–13
research 21–2, 66, 70–1
resources 33, 39, 56, 84–5, 94, 98, 101–03
respect 72, 87, 101, 122; inclusion 11–13, 15–16, 24, 35, 40; staff 51–3, 111–15, 117
responsibility 27, 72, 84, 99, 114–17
rhymes 58, 62, 101
risks 44–7, 55, 59, 62
role models 107, 114
role play 56–7, 60, 64, 79, 84, 105
rotas 110–11, 114, 122–24
routines 90–1
rules 28, 68–9, 98

safeguarding 31, 48
safety 26–8, 40–3, 47–50, 58, 98–9

salaries 27, 124
sand 19, 56, 64
schemas 62, 64–6, 70
schools 96, 130, 132–33, 135–36
secretary 27
security 45
self-care *see* independence
self-confidence 1, 8–9, 23, 35, 88, 102, 135
self-esteem 15, 124
SEN 38–9
SENCOs 38, 100
SEND 37–9
sensory impairments 18, 26, 61, 93–4
separation anxiety 86
services 97, 100, 106
sessions 28, 52, 94, 102, 105
shifts 123
siblings 3–4, 67, 77, 136
signing 15, 18, 47, 94
skills 1, 5, 23, 34, 76, 105, 126
small world play 56–7
social media 119
Social Services 49, 98
songs 62, 84, 101
special needs 7, 37–9, 47, 53, 92–4, 116–17
specialist professionals 86–7, 90, 94, 100
speech therapist 86
staff 26–8, 31, 39, 51; appreciation 112–14; meetings 118; organisation 120–22; responsibilities 114–19, 122–126; roles 97–193; service 108–09; specialist 100–01; timekeeping 109–12
Statutory Framework *see* EYFS
stories 19, 58, 60, 62, 101
students 98, 102, 105–06
supervision 50, 94, 98–100, 105, 114–16
supply staff 50, 90, 98–100, 125

Index

support 1, 24, 34; families 87, 89–90; 100, 116, 132–33; language 16, 20; staff 50–4, 105, 109

tantrums 79, 88
teachers 67, 73, 92, 135–36
teaching assistants 73, 88
teamwork 62, 104, 109
thanks 5, 112–13, 125, 136
themes 55, 74, 85
theory 70–1, 103
tidying up 62, 93, 110–11, 120–22, 132
timekeeping 50, 109–12
timetables 97, 111
toddlers 24, 35, 67, 94, 105
toilet training 13, 87–8

toys 32, 84–5, 98, 101
training 124; families 19; staff 26, 31, 34, 48, 50, 98, 103–06, 115
transitions 96, 130–38
translation 8, 15–16, 20, 101, 105
treasurer 27
trips *see* outings

Understanding the World 60–1

visitors 96, 99, 135–36
visual impairment 18, 93
volunteers 48, 98–100, 105, 125
vouchers 28

water 19, 56, 60–1, 64
working patterns 5–6